I0103797

Alexei Anisin

Authoritarian Liberal Surveillance and the COVID-19 Pandemic

De Gruyter Contemporary Social Sciences

—

Volume 25

Alexei Anisin

Authoritarian Liberal Surveillance and the COVID-19 Pandemic

—

DE GRUYTER

ISBN 978-3-11-163102-8
e-ISBN (PDF) 978-3-11-134570-3
e-ISBN (EPUB) 978-3-11-134593-2
ISSN 2747-5689
e-ISSN 2747-5697

Library of Congress Control Number: 2023944012

Bibliographic information published by the Deutsche Nationalbibliothek
The Deutsche Nationalbibliothek lists this publication in the Deutsche Nationalbibliografie;
detailed bibliographic data are available on the Internet at http://dnb.dnb.de.

© 2024 Walter de Gruyter GmbH, Berlin/Boston
This volume is text- and page-identical with the hardback published in 2024.
Cover image: da-kuk / E+ / Getty Images

www.degruyter.com

Contents

Chapter 1: Introduction

Introduction

Incoming fog pours over gothic architectural marvels on a cold and dark afternoon in what just months prior was one of Central Europe's most lively and visited cities. Parking spots along narrow cobblestoned streets are empty and the atmosphere is strangely eerie. Sirens can be heard somewhere in the distance, fading out. Shops are closed and few pedestrians pass by streets that are usually bustling with energy and noise. It's January of 2021 in Prague and state instilled restrictions due to the COVID-19 pandemic are in full swing – civilians are not allowed to leave the precinct of either the city, town, or village they reside in. The COVID-19 pandemic had a profound impact on the entirety of 2020, 2021, and the early portion of 2022. State-enforced regulations on social behavior and movement were active across much of the world and constituted among the largest, if not the largest, governmental-led shutdowns of socio-economic activity in human history. Schools, universities, public venues, sports facilities, travel hubs, and many other social and cultural places were shut. Billions of people shifted their life into online modes of communication. While parents were on conference and work calls on digital applications such as Zoom or Microsoft Teams, their children were concurrently on similar platforms, being instructed by teachers who would attempt to draw out homework instructions on blurry whiteboards. Food and essential goods were purchased in a highly regulated manner – apart from corporate super market retail chains, the height of the pandemic saw small shops, businesses, and restaurants getting orders to close their doors or change their mode of product delivery to consumers (Anisin, 2022a).

The rapid onset of the pandemic was marked by a sense of collective panic and uncertainty. For months at a time across most countries in the world, it was not legal to leave one's accommodation and area of residence without an N95 face-mask, a surgical mask, or a home-made cloth mask. Social gatherings were banned or limited to particular sizes of groups and into latter waves of the pandemic, it was not possible to participate in social activities without proof of vaccination or a negative medical test. Describing the varying outcomes and tendencies that arose during the pandemic may now seem to be reflective of a normal cognizant activity – we all remember what happened and recognize the severity that the first emergent strains of the COVID-19 virus posed for at-risk subsets of populations. The pandemic had a profound dislocatory impact on social affairs and although we are only three years removed from its onset, thousands of scientific studies and hundreds of books on this topic have either already been published or are in the proc-

https://doi.org/10.1515/9783111345703-001

ess of peer review. The sheer frequency with which the pandemic has been researched by scholars is indicative of the profound transformative effects it brought about for many societies across the world.

If we take a step back and attempt to generalize about how our world sometimes tends to change before our eyes, we will eventually come up against the observation that political history is commonly driven by incremental changes that arise through institutional bargaining and legislation, through technological changes, but every few decades, events of incredible global significance arise and when such events arise, they tend to surpass many preceding events in their impact on social structures. World wars, civil wars, revolutions, natural disasters, and economic depressions tend to take up the most space in history textbooks and these events are generally accepted by populations around the world as phenomena that constitute regular trajectories of social change. Recent years have revealed that a pandemic not only has the propensity to be considered as an event alongside the aforementioned phenomena, but can supplant them in terms of sheer causal impact. Lockdowns and pandemic-related restrictions have been related to economic activities, economic growth, political trust, social trust, political polarization, numerous health outcomes, mental health, suicide, drug usage, addictions, domestic violence, environmental pollution, consumption patterns, shopping behavior, food intake, protest, schooling and learning outcomes, among many other topics. This book draws attention to the political, economic, and social implications of the pandemic – it adopts two different conceptual frameworks of authoritarian liberalism and surveillance capitalism. In doing so, I demonstrate that the pandemic began as a set of crises that were sparked by a genuine epidemiological emergency, but as time went on, crises became propagated for political and economic purposes.

There are many different routes and approaches that one could take to study the pandemic. This book is concerned with what I believe to be among the more important topics – that of making sense of the political implications that pandemic policies have on the standing of liberal democracy. Although the pandemic was a common point of discussion in public discourse throughout English speaking countries during 2020, 2021, and to some extent 2022, as time has gone on, it seems that it is largely starting to be looked back on as a highly negative point in recent human history for a plethora of different reasons. It has since been revealed that many of the restrictions and mandates that were enforced upon populations were not as effective as they were marketed to be by policy makers and in the most extreme of cases, policy makers and political elites themselves did not abide by restrictions that they enforced upon the rest of society (e.g., Boris Johnson's "Partygate" banquets or Czech Health Minister Roman Prymula's maskless attendance of football matches during lockdown). By March of 2023, there were an estimated 6,881,955 million global fatalities attributed to COVID-19 and upwards of 676,609,955 detected cases according to the John Hopkins COVID-19 dashboard tracker (Center for Systems Science and Engineering, 2023). Data drawn from the U.S. Centers for Disease Control and Prevention (CDC) reveals that the year 2020 saw an estimated 351,913 deaths from COVID-19 and the median age of Americans who succumbed to the virus was 78 years old. Similar data from the CDC for 2021 indicates that the median age of COVID-19 induced fatalities was 74 years old. Pezzullo et. al's (2023) inquiry (29 countries) on age-stratified infection fatality rates of COVID-19 revealed that in non-elderly populations, the virus was not very lethal – 0–19: years old 0.0003 %; 20–29: 0.002 %; 30–39: 0.011 %; 40–49: 0.035 %; 50–59: 0.123 %; 60–69: 0.0506 %; 0–69: 0.063–0.082 %.

While the aim of this book is not to assess the epidemiological value that restrictions may have on population health, it is important to recognize that public policies which were created to attempt to deal with the spreading of a respiratory virus ended up constituting the most profound restrictions on civil liberties, human behavior, and social interactions in the history of liberal democracy if observed cross-nationally. Very few (if any) empirical phenomena have had the type of impact that the pandemic has on human affairs and social organization. Unpacking the potential causal impact that pandemic policies had on different political, economic, and social outcomes can shed light on some of the most important political forces that are at play in our current historical era. The pandemic fostered a massive dislocation to social, political, and economic structures, and just as in previous historical instances of dislocation, most countries saw power holding groups utilize moments of political contingency for their own benefit. These dynamics were not driven or brought about by the commonly referenced explanatory frameworks of democratic backsliding and populism. Deeper forces were at play – forces that hovered in the background and constituted antecedent authoritarian liberal and surveillance capitalistic processes.

Making Sense of Pandemic Restrictions

A primary hypothesis that led me to write this book pertained to my observations of different political and economic consequences of pandemic policies. In 2020 it already appeared to me that many liberal democracies had undergone a metamorphosis – across liberal democratic contexts, governments engaged in the unfettered implementation of surveillance alongside authoritarian liberal policy making. Governments pleased corporate interests and meanwhile, greatly contributed to public debt through printing trillions of dollars to bail out different industries. Emergency relief in places such as Canada or the United States saw monthly checks going out to citizens that hovered around $2000 per month. This money, paradoxically, ended up in the pockets of corporate actors because concurrent policies governments and ministries of health took ended up favoring large-capacity retail chains who were deemed as providers of "essential goods." Stimulus checks not only depoliticized masses of people from engaging in collective action, but they also brought about a classical authoritarian liberal strategy of insulating the economy from democratic pressures (Wilkinson, 2021; 2022).

As most liberal democracies saw incumbent governments print trillions of dollars and disproportionately add to their country's national debt to favor corporate interests over workers, middle classes, and small to medium sized businesses, newfangled industries entered the "too big to fail" category that was once relevant for corporate banks and the automotive industry in the United States. Corporate retail shopping chains profited greatly as did pharmaceutical corporations. The pandemic saw rich countries across the world fail to increase taxes on the richest of their citizens and concurrently public goods such as vaccine science were privatized (Oxfam International, 2022). This led to an intensification of monopolization and market concentration in these spheres which ended up being greater in just one year (2020) than in all years from 2000–15. It is estimated that globally, governments spent $16 trillion as a response to the pandemic. This astronomical total was not spent evenly nor was it distributed to all sectors of the economy in an equal manner. According to Oxfam International (2022) the pandemic led to a surge in inequality, and the ten richest people doubled their fortunes (from $700 billion to $1.5 trillion) during the first two years. Inequality brought about by the pandemic and associated policies was estimated to have killed at least 21,000 people per day across the world. Director of Oxfam International, Gabriela Butcher notably stated,

> Billionaires have had a terrific pandemic. Central banks pumped trillions of dollars into financial markets to save the economy, yet much of that has ended up lining the pockets of billionaires riding a stock market boom. Vaccines were meant to end this pandemic, yet rich governments allowed pharma billionaires and monopolies to cut off the supply to billions of people. The result is that every kind of inequality imaginable risks rising. The predictability of it is sickening. The consequences of it kill (Oxfam International, 2022).

A key dynamic that I observed throughout the development, or evolution, of the pandemic, was that policies that were enforced throughout the course of 2020, 2021, and the beginning portion of 2022 would not have been possible without antecedent conditions that stem to surveillance capitalism. Technological corporations shared their platforms with state security institutions to monitor, quarantine, trace, and place entire populations under surveillance. This book explores how such outcomes arose and argues that pandemic responses in liberal democratic states were premised on an array of incongruities and illiberal practices that arose through governments' exercising of political power over vast swaths of geographic space, people, and institutions. Pandemic policies fostered the largest lockdowns, quarantines, and restrictions in modern human history if viewed across liberal democratic societies. In order to uphold one fundamental function of liberal democratic social order (the protection of human life), governments carried out policies that severely infringed, and in many instances, violated other aspects of liberal democratic socio-political order and institutional checks and balances. In multiple ways, the pandemic fostered a plethora of "illiberal practices" if observed through the guise of Glasius' (2018) framework. The same can be said with regard to how illiberal practices manifested in what scholars have recently described as a rapidly evolving "digital sphere" (Glasius & Michaelsen, 2018).

The many different policies that were enforced by states during the course of the pandemic functioned through either emergency decrees or during state of emergencies. In most cases, the lines between constitutional legality and democratic norms were blurred and erratic. Soft laws were widely utilized and parliaments were frequently inattentive to review of legislation for variant reasons. Through analysis of a sample of liberal democratic states (n=54), this book reveals that apart from less than a handful of countries, pandemic responses in liberal democracies were driven by authoritarian liberalist functions and were likewise reliant on surveillance capitalistic structures and technologies. Importantly, the synthesis between authoritarian liberalism and surveillance capitalism that arose throughout the pandemic was significant but also variant. Not all countries took on authoritarian liberal approaches to the pandemic and not all countries placed their populaces under heavy surveillance. Most however, did, including countries that not only makeup some of the largest economies in the world, but countries that tend to receive praise in rankings across democracy measures and datasets.

This book situates authoritarian liberal policies that were put forward to deal with the pandemic alongside a larger historical trajectory of authoritarian liberalism which dates back to Weimar Germany. The implications of this argument are twofold. First, in contrast to an emerging wave of scholarship that is currently prevalent across social science, democratically adverse policies that arose during the pandemic were not driven by populism or democratic backsliding. Second, in contrast to the 2007–8 global financial crisis and the 2011 Eurozone crisis, both of which were heavily impacted by authoritarian liberalist policies (Wilkinson, 2021), the pandemic fostered overtly authoritarian liberal policies that evolved in real time according to conditions that came along with each of the five waves. These tendencies varied across the sample of cases as observable via different restrictions, bailouts, stimulus packages, and legislative behavior. Throughout these processes, different actors and groups benefited greatly at the expense of others

– especially working and middle classes. A key difference between how authoritarian liberalism manifested during the pandemic in comparison to previous eras (such as the 2007–8 global recession or the 2011 Eurozone crisis) can be observed in the supplementary role that surveillance capitalism played in its synthesis with state security institutions.

During the pandemic, surveillance capitalistic structures were complimentary to governments and state institutions – they enabled authorities to monitor, quarantine, and track populations. In other words, data architecture and technology that hitherto belonged to the realm of surveillance capitalism was drawn upon by governments and state security institutions to enforce pandemic restrictions. Into the third and fourth waves of the pandemic, QR codes were widely utilized as a method of social control – these mechanisms operated through surveillance capitalistic platforms in order to enforce authoritarian liberal policies across most social and economic spheres of human activity. Surveillance capitalism also facilitated entire populations to acquiesce to using digital technology to work, go to school, interact, and get entertained. In previous research (Anisin 2022a;b;c) I investigated these dynamics mainly in the context of the European Union (EU). In this book my analysis is expanded in theoretical terms and in empirical scope.

Authoritarian Liberalism and Surveillance Capitalism

Explaining adverse outcomes and processes that arose during the pandemic can be done through many different frameworks and just as any given socio-political topic, there is no exact or factually precise approach that should be adopted to analyze and research this subject. This book engages with the following literatures through the prism of the pandemic: surveillance capitalism [defined as hidden commercial practices of extraction, prediction and a rogue mutation of capitalism marked by concentrations of wealth, knowledge, and power that claim a uniliteral monopoly over human experience based on the foundation of a surveillance economy (Zuboff, 2019)]; democratic backsliding [defined as a deterioration of qualities associated with democratic governance; a decline in the quality of democracy (Walder & Lust, 2018)], populism [defined as "a thin-centered ideology that considers society to be ultimately separated into two homogenous and antagonistic groups: "the pure people" and "the corrupt elite," and argues that politics should be an expression of the volonté générale (general will) of the people" (Mudde, 2004)], and authoritarian liberalism [premised around the classical liberal belief that a society must be based on competition and exchange combined with a belief that a given state's functions must not be impeded by democratic architecture and potential blockades that prevent it from enforcing pro-market efficiency in major economic and policy outcomes (Wilkinson, 2021, p. 27)].

While scholars have thus far produced an impressive amount of research on the pandemic and have diligently paid attention to its impact on a range of outcomes including the international system (Anisin, 2021), social behavior (Bigo, Guild, & Kuskonmaz, 2021), surveillance (Sweeney, 2020; Treguer, 2020; 2021; Zorina et al., 2021), and the adversities that restrictions had on democratic institutions (Csernatoni, 2020; Eichler & Sonkar, 2021), there has yet to be a critical cross-national inquiry carried out into the ramifications that restriction policies produced for liberal democratic standing. At the time of writing this book, scholars from different institutions, countries, and disciplinary backgrounds are starting to hint that a form of democratic erosion did indeed arise during the pandemic. Edgell, Lachapelle, Luhrmann, & Maerz (2021) find that both illiberal and authoritarian practices were not correlated with better public health outcomes as observed across 144 countries (drawn from the PanDem dataset). Lockdowns and limitation on movement or assembly rights were interpreted as being in violation of democratic standards if they were disproportionate, discriminatory, or abusively enforced. In contrast, in an econometric analysis, Lewkowicz, Wozniak, & Wrzesinski (2022) find that the direct violations of democracy were less likely to occur with relation to the strength of democratic institutions and the rule of law.

Some have argued that populists and populist supporters were likelier to oppose restriction policies and promote conspiracies associated with the pandemic (Eberl, Huber, & Greussing, 2021). It is regularly said that if adverse policies did arise due to pandemic restrictions or regulations, then such policies run risk of adding to a longer stemming dynamic of democratic erosion that is argued to have manifested over the last decade or so. What such approaches fail to consider however, is that there is variance in how high-ranking democratic polities dealt with the pandemic. For example, Sweden took a very different approach to dealing with restriction recommendations and lockdowns than Australia, yet both are similarly ranked in democratic measures and data sets if observed across the years of the pandemic (e. g., V-Dem, Freedom House). What's more, some of the most "populistic" statements made by political leaders can be observed in countries that took on among the harshest measures to deal with the pandemic (e. g., Australia or Canada). To date, analyses of the pandemic have not been able to account for multifaceted sets of illiberal tendencies that arose throughout liberal democratic states over the course of nearly three turbulent years.

Another problem in social scientific scholarship on the pandemic pertains to how scholars have tended to select on the dependent variable by placing focus on a set of countries that are already designated as either authoritarian or populistic and then observing adverse epidemiological outcomes in the said country or set of countries. For instance, in a recently published monograph, *Populists and the Pandemic*, Ringe & Renno (2023) put forward an interesting analysis of populist leaders and governance strategies during the pandemic, yet as common in research on populism, analyses tend to be representative of an "n=1" and the mistake of selecting on the dependent variable (populism) is made. There is much greater complexity and variance inherent to political and economic processes that arose during the pandemic than aforementioned approaches can account for. In a similar vein, if scholars place focus on one single analytical or theoretical framework, then this runs risk of taking away our ability to be able to look at the bigger picture of social, economic, and political phenomena that arose during a given historical time period.

This book argues that the pandemic was marked and dominated by two processes – authoritarian liberalism and surveillance capitalism. Throughout the pandemic, these processes surfaced and merged with one another and contributed to what arguably were the largest collection of illiberal practices in the history of liberal democracy.

Methodological Approach

This book takes a multi-methodological approach to assess pandemic restrictions and policies throughout 54 different states. Addressing and explaining one of the more polarizing topics of our times requires a careful mode of inquiry that is conceptually multifaceted and not contingent on any single framework. This book draws from two different frameworks and many data reference points to carry out comparative inquiry on COVID-19 policies. In detail, I analyze the following countries: Austria, Belgium, Brazil, Bulgaria, Canada, Croatia, Cyprus, Czech Republic, Denmark, Estonia, Finland, France, Germany, Greece, Hungary, Iceland, Ireland, Israel, Italy, Jamaica, Japan, Latvia, Lithuania, Malta, Mexico, Netherlands, Norway, Poland, Portugal, Romania, Slovak Republic, Slovenia, South Korea, Spain, Sweden, Switzerland, United Kingdom, United States, Argentina, Australia ,Barbados, Chile, Cape Verde, Costa Rica, Ghana, New Zealand, Panama, Peru, Senegal, South Africa, Taiwan, Trinidad and Tobago, Uruguay, Paraguay. The heterogeneity inherent to the countries under attention is beneficial from a methodological point of view because it provides us with variance in terms of the independent variables in the research design and the overall statistical analyses carried out in this book.

Throughout the empirical portions of this book, I draw on different datasets and sources to assess particular policies and to identify quantitative trends across the cases under attention. The methodological analyses in this book involve case studies, comparative case studies, and quantitative and statistical inquiry. After a literature review in which I highlight numerous social inquiries which have been carried out on the pandemic, I delve into a theoretical overview of the concepts found in aforementioned frameworks used to study the status of liberal democracy and the various ways in which it can be measured. Subsequently, I carry out a temporally sensitive analysis of each of the five waves of the pandemic. Here every country's contact tracing application is identified along with its date of implementation. The same methodological strategy is adopted to identify the names of COVID-19 health certificates across each country. To contextualize these developments, a case study of pandemic policies in the Czech Republic is carried out – here, documents, policy reports, information such as court hearings, trials, and other government produced information on policies during the pandemic are analyzed. Reference is given to other countries in the sample of cases as well. The analysis is chronological and begins in the first month of 2020 then shifts into the different waves of the pandemic. As waves one, two, and three were by far the most lethal, the highest frequency of restrictions were carried out by governments during this time.

In the succeeding parts of my empirical analysis, I utilize quantitative methodology to investigate the 54 cases that form the sample analyzed in this book. Here, descriptive statistics are utilized to overview populational and demographic information for each country; GDP per capita; average life expectancy; percentage of vaccinated adults with relation to total COVID-19 fatalities; the initiation of state of emergencies. Data on QR code usage and electronic vaccination or health certificates are analyzed for each country. Along with these data, I draw from the Oxford COVID-19 Government Response Tracker (OxCGRT) (Blavatnik School of Government, 2022) to assess aggregations of policy responses according to a stringency index that is based on nine different indicators. Data on states of emergencies in each country are provided along with vaccination percentage estimates and total virus-induced fatality estimates. The main component of this book's empirical analysis features a quantitative investigation of democratic rankings through three different datasets including the years 2019, 2020, 2021, and 2022 to identify whether democratic rankings significantly changed in the noted years as a result of pandemic policies. The datasets include the Economist's Intelligence Unit Democracy Rankings; V-Dem; Freedom House. The inquiry is then proceeded by a look into estimated excess mortality rates for all countries for the year 2020, with data drawn from the Human Mortality Database.

The final part of this book's empirical analyses is on authoritarian liberal policies as observed in bailouts and stimulus packages. Corporate profiteering during the pandemic was significant, and in some cases, was induced by restrictions and policies that lent great support to specific industries whether through bailouts, stimulus packages, or through partial economic shutdowns. Here, I provide data for the 54 countries under attention on their Gini Coefficient (a measure of the level inequality in a given society) as well as their national debt percentage relative to GDP. This is followed by an examination of corporate tax rates in each country with relation to the highest individual income tax bracket rate. Afterwards, data are presented with estimates on the total amount each country spent on COVID-19 bailouts and stimulus packages. A comparative analysis of airline and auto industry bailouts is then provided, with emphasis being placed on a range of different cases from the sample. A similar qualitative approach is then drawn on to investigate corporate supermarket retail chains. Finally, the conclusion of this book offers a reflective overview of restrictions that implemented in the pandemic with relation to different health, social, and economic outcomes through overviews of post-pandemic epidemiological studies and several meta-analyses.

Order of Chapters

The order of contents of this book are as follows: the second chapter provides readers with a comprehensive overview of the four theoretical frameworks that are compared and contrasted throughout this book: authoritarian liberalism, surveillance capitalism, populism, and democratic backsliding. Central assumptions and findings stemming to literature on democratic backsliding and populism are presented. The third chapter identifies different trajectories of authoritarian liberalism that have arisen over the course of the last century; delves into different forms of surveillance and traces recent developments of surveillance capitalism as observed across high profile political events. Afterwards, the key assumptions of the book are put forward and categorized. This is followed by an explanation of the research design of this book and its multi-methodological nature.

Next, chapter four presents temporally sensitive classifications of five waves of the pandemic beginning with wave one, then moving onto waves two, three, four, and five. The chapter also includes a brief explanation on the history of pandemics and infectious diseases. It then presents readers with a quantitative overview of each country's stringency index as gauged through data drawn from Oxford Coronavirus Government Response Tracker. Alongside these data, the chapter presents readers with information on contact tracing applications along with COVID-19 health certificates as observed across each country. A case study is then carried out through the qualitative context of the Czech Republic, reference is given to other cases as well. The analysis provides an intriguing viewpoint into the complexity of implications that pandemic policies pose for liberal democracy. The chapter finishes with an inquiry into latter waves of the pandemic in which QR codes, digital health certificates, and other similar tools of surveillance were widely adopted by states to regulate human behavior and social interactions. These dynamics are revealed to have been made possible by surveillance capitalistic structures which were utilized to favor authoritarian liberal social and economic policies.

Chapter five begins with a quick look into data on vaccination percentage estimates as observed across all countries in the sample (data drawn from the New York Times' COVID Vaccine Tracker) which are then related to data drawn from the WHO's cumulative tracking estimates on COVID-19 fatalities. The chapter then provides what is, to the best of my knowledge, the first comprehensive look into state of emergencies as observed across a large portion of liberal democratic states. This analysis is complimented by inquiry into the concept of a soft law and an explanation of how such legislation became prominent during the pandemic. Here, it is revealed that across most countries in the sample, policies averse to the standing of liberal democracy were not random, but were reliant on legislation that was enacted while putting forward restriction and quarantine policies through state of emergencies, by variant types of emergency powers acts, or by way of non-binding soft laws. These policies were complimented by the merger of state and corporate-led surveillance of civilians which functioned through electronic and digital based tracking systems. The fifth chapter then provides an overview of data and measures of democracy that are commonly utilized throughout the aforementioned literature in social scientific inquiry on democracy and authoritarianism. Differences in how democracy is classified and categorized are explicated through identification of variables that are commonly associated with democracy including elections, media freedom, institutional characteristics, and civil liberties. The chapter analyzes three datasets. It then shifts to an explanation which offers readers a preliminary set of examples about how a number of key measures of democracy stemming to these three datasets were violated and infringed upon during the pandemic. It demonstrates that at height of the pandemic (waves one and two), there was an interplay between surveillance and restrictions which varied according to context and country, and although monitoring civilians' health status through digital technology is not a completely new phenomenon, the implementation of surveillance monitoring tools during COVID-19 far surpassed any previous era in liberal democracy history in scope. The chapter finishes with an overview of estimated excess mortality rates as observed across all countries in the sample for the year 2020.

Chapter six delves into a heterogeneous collection of economic policies that accompanied pandemic restriction guidelines. The chapter reveals that economic policies were carried out in nearly a uniform manner across liberal democratic countries during not only the height of the pandemic, but also into its later waves. Countries printed billions (and some, even trillions) to put forward stimulus and bailout packages. Through rescuing corporate industries, governments added to their country's national debt, and meanwhile, some corporate industries flourished. Very specific authoritarian liberal policies were put forward in attempt to optimize particular corporate industries through classification of "essential goods" providers. Not only did economic processes and attempted redistribution of large amounts of money that governments printed end up in corporate hands, but public debt and inflation skyrocketed and masses of people were depoliticized as a result of pandemic restriction policies. The chapter also presents data on QR code regulations which were active across most of the sample of cases under attention.

The final chapter, chapter seven, summarizes the findings of the empirical analyses that were carried out throughout this book. The chapter highlights the different types of authoritarian liberal responses that were at play throughout the pandemic. Apart from less than a handful of countries (out of the 54 under attention), governments' responses to the pandemic were illiberal, overly restrictive, and comparatively unparalleled when related to health responses in previous eras of modern history. The overarching findings of this book compliment Wilkinson's recent work on authoritarian liberalism, but in doing so, point attention to a commonly neglected point of interest in this literature – that authoritarian liberalism is an ever-evolving and mutating phenomenon. The pandemic revealed how this phenomenon synthesized with surveillance capitalism. In support of these claims, the chapter presents readers with a set of conclusions that begin with health-based outcomes that have since been revealed after the end of the pandemic. The chapter ends with a discussion of implications and presents several directions that can be taken on in future social inquiry.

Chapter 2: Is the World Becoming more Illiberal?

Introduction

A doctor is pictured sitting on the ground with her head against the wall in the early hours of morning. Patient beds extend outwards into the hallway of a crowded intensive care unit. Beds are placed alongside the walls of a corridor. Wearing double, and in some cases, even triple surgical masks, doctors and nurses hover in the background and appear to be panicking. Its March of 2020 and the first wave of the pandemic is in full swing. The entire year thus far has been dominated by the story of COVID-19, its emergence, and its rapid spread throughout the world. News headlines across the English-speaking world present audiences with sensationalist headlines of topics such as "Coronavirus 'tsunami' pushes Italy's hospitals to breaking point" (Johnson & Ghiglione, 2020), "INSIDE ITALY'S COVID WAR" (Achilli & Edge, 2020), "Italy has a world-class health system. The coronavirus has pushed it to the breaking point" (Chow & Saliba, 2020), or "18 Years Old and on a Ventilator With COVID-19" (Taddonio, 2020). The 24/7 news cycle far surpasses anything resembling the classical 1990s' "CNN effect" – as headlines, retweets, shares, and online communication surrounding pandemic stories infiltrate social media networks at a rapid pace and form the basis of discussions for hundreds of millions, if not billions of people around the world. Even the most prestigious of outlets in natural science such as *The Lancet*, put out commentaries (in March of 2020) titled, "The Italian war-like measures to fight coronavirus spreading: Re-open closed hospitals now" (Miani et al., 2020).

Three years later, readers will likely recall that Italy was the first liberal democratic state to have experienced a heavy concentration of cases of COVID-19 – at the height of the first wave of the pandemic. It was also among the first states (apart from China and other East Asian countries) to instill strict lockdown measures across its society. Retrospectively, having lived through and followed news cycles during 9/11, the Iraq War, the 2007–8 financial crisis, the election of Donald Trump in 2016, all of these events paled in comparison to the pandemic in terms of the sheer frequency of reports that were put out, the extent of discussions that accompanied them, and above all, the extent of anxiety and uncertainty that ensued once sensationalist news reporting started to pick up stories of overcrowded ICUs and the "war" efforts that were ongoing on the "frontline" and "battlefield" against COVID-19. Responses to the pandemic were unprecedented in terms of the sheer scope of surveillance that was placed on civilians' health statuses, the extent of restrictions that were utilized in attempt to control human behavior, and the abruptness with which daily life changed for billions of people throughout the world.

https://doi.org/10.1515/9783111345703-002

The pandemic has posed many intriguing questions about the nature of political power in an era that scholars contend as is marked by either populism, democratic erosion, or a combination of both. This chapter will demonstrate why both of these noted frameworks fall short in being able to account for adverse outcomes that arose during the pandemic. In doing so, it will provide an in-depth overview of research findings that stem to both of these literatures. Afterwards, I will introduce the frameworks of authoritarian liberalism and surveillance capitalism.

Democratic Backsliding

In an increasingly salient literature, scholars have examined ailments that democratic polities have experienced over the last two decades. This literature is referred to as "democratic backsliding" or simply, "backsliding" and tends to be concerned with institutional corrosion. While some quantitative inquiries have been carried out on backsliding, comparative case studies are most common, with the European Union context serving as an expected forefront for observing backsliding, especially countries such as Hungary or Poland. As a reoccurring empirical phenomenon, democratic backsliding is a tricky one to define because it tends to be observed in temporally elongated form that is comprised of a series of events and processes, rather than a one-shot outcome. Waldner & Lust (2018) describe democratic backsliding as a phenomenon that is incremental in nature and not a "coup de grace" (Walder & Lust, 2018, p. 95). However, as noted by Bermeo (2016), although backsliding is a frequently used term, its substance is rarely analyzed through a critical guise. Similarly, Glasius puts forward a plausible set of claims in noting that, "But professional political scientists can give little guidance as to whether there are such things as 'everyday acts of authoritarianism' or 'autocratic leadership' in a democratic society, and if so what they would look like." Further noting that, "we lack the vocabulary and the tools to provide a clear, research-based analysis of these apparent phenomena of authoritarianism and illiberalism within established democracies' (Glasius, 2018, p. 515–16).

Wolkenstein's (2022) recent recommendations for understanding democratic backsliding on a qualitative level are worth considering. Here, it is noted that scholars must, "1) explain why particular developments constitute a degeneration of democracy (rather than simply stating that they are a degeneration of democracy), which presupposes that it can, 2) identify democratic regressions without resorting to a Eurocentric developmental view of history, while 3), resisting the temptation to overgeneralize the place and function of particular ideal-typical features of democracy (as "models of democracy"-approaches usually do) (Wolkenstein, 2022, p. 4).

Democratic performance has been analyzed through observation of how incumbent leaders and political parties behave or whether civilians support democracy and its norms and values. There are also a number of approaches that have associated backsliding with global political processes based around nation states' behaviors and interests. The underlying assumptions of this literature are historically rooted – democracy and political institutions have been studied for arguably the longest period of time when compared to other phenomena in political science. The first systematic projects that surveyed citizens in the 1940s "revolutionized social science" and changed democratic societies because they provided a new gold standard for measuring citizen opinions which are at the heart of democratic deliberation (Brady, 2000, p. 47). Since the historical trajectory of social inquiry on democracy and political institutions has swayed towards survey research and gauging citizen discontent with their political representatives, it is thus not surprising that the most influential of studies on democratic backsliding have principally placed emphasis on interactions that take place between electorates, the elected, and political institutions.

Foa & Mounk's (2016) study was among the early inquiries that sparked interest in democratic erosion. Here, public opinion data were analyzed and the analysis revealed that citizens of wealthy established democracies are less satisfied with government than ever before. The authors argued that a "serious democratic disconnect has emerged," and that this disconnect may have enough proclivity to challenge consolidated democracies. A fascinating aspect of the inquiry can be observed in their visualization of world values survey evidence in which respondents were asked whether it is "essential" to live in a country that is governed democratically. The figure's Y axis featured percentiles (ranging from 30 to 80 %) and the X axis featured birth cohort decades (ranging from the 1930s to the 1980s). The data reveal an astonishing downward trend for both the US and Europe. In the former, for respondents that were born in the 1930s, close to 75 % believed living in a democratic country was essential – for those born in the 1980s, just above 30 % held the same beliefs. The aggregation of European citizens' responses is a bit different, with a peak occurring in the generation that was born in the 1950s (to close to 60 %), then a downward trend leading to around 45 % for those born in the 1980s. Foa & Mounk (2016) describe these findings as "deeply concerning" because citizens from "supposedly consolidates democracies" across North America and Western Europe are not only critical of their political leadership, but are cynical about the value of democracy has as a political system. In turn, this has resulted in large amounts of people losing hope that they can influence public policy.

Another piece of the puzzle of democratic erosion pertains to citizens' growing support of authoritarianism. The aforementioned study found that both upper-income and lower and middle-income respondents experienced an increase in support for authoritarianism from the period of 1995 to around 2007–8, then onwards, only upper-income respondents continued to experience an increase in support for authoritarianism, while lower and middle-income respondents experienced a slight drop. The latter drop however, was found to be marginal as only around 32% of these respondents still expressed support for authoritarianism (data were up until the year 2014). The normative implications of this study were profound because it represented arguably the first investigation that identified the incredibly significant trend of young peoples' dissatisfaction with democracy in advanced liberal democratic societies.

In contrast to Foa & Mounk's inquiry, several high-profile inquiries have put forward counter arguments which posit that democracy in advanced liberal democratic societies is not on the decline, and that citizens still heavily aspire towards democratic norms and values (Norris, 2011). Wuttke, Gavras, & Schoen (2020) investigate survey evidence from 18 European countries (spanning 1981–2018) and find that while there are adversities with younger generations' support for democracy, citizens by and large still heavily support and endorse self-governance. With this being said, it appears that more and more scholars are adding to the democratic erosion hypothesis. Svolik (2019) attributes problems in electorates to democratic backsliding. In a widely cited article, the author contends that political polarization has undermined democracy through several key mechanisms. In explaining the backdrop of the rise of authoritarianism, the author takes on a similar approach as found in aforementioned studies. First, backsliding is accounted for by the agency of elite actors or groups through either coups or executive takeovers – both of which have contributed to 197 total democratic "downgrades" over the course of 1973–2018. Prior to the end of the Cold War, nearly all democratic breakdowns occurred as a result of military coups, yet in the post-Cold War era, the frequency of executive-based takeovers surged (Slovik, 2019). A key characteristic of the latter, claims Slovik, can be observed in relative levels of popular support that incumbent authoritarian leaders acquire and uphold throughout their rule. This leads Slovik to reason that political polarization is associated to a historical surge of executive takeovers. If a population is polarized and political cleavages result in divergences and partisan-based interests, a given electorate will be unable to serve as a democratic check because voters will be willing to "trade off democratic principles for partisan interests," argues Svolik. Since voters may be reluctant to "punish" politicians (through electoral mechanisms) and if pursuing democratic principles requires abandoning their favored party preferences, then this can result in low rates of electoral feedback for undemocratic political behavior on the part of elites.

An issue with this argument, however, is that it is premised on outdated assumptions that do not capture empirical processes of surveillance that have arisen in the last two decades. The reality is that societies are under heavy surveillance from both political and non-political actors, and political parties in liberal democratic states have repeatedly privileged corporate interests, favored market outcomes, manipulated public debt, and have depoliticized masses during periods of economic downturn. As the sixth chapter of this book will reveal, policy makers added more to governments' debt in the period of two fiscal years (2020 and 2021) than nearly all previous single comparable periods of economic crisis. At the same time, some governments sent stimulus checks to individuals through the mail according different parameters, which in turn, kept political grievances from forming into anti-governmental movements and revolutionary ideas.

Furthermore, in research on backsliding, another key set of characteristics have been observed. Here, literature on democratic norms and citizen opinions has to do with individual incentives and preferences that individuals may have for violating democratic values. Krishnarajan (2022) argues that even though prior research has demonstrated that individual preferences and decision making can align with undemocratic actions and behaviors, such outcomes only arise out of non-deliberate rationalization in which citizens form beliefs that undemocratic actions are actually democratic through what the author describes as "perception bias." Political cleavages are also significantly relatable to democratic erosion and as readers will likely acknowledge, many of history's greatest diversions in democratic polities occurred as a result of cleavages and antagonisms that were held by either a majority ethnic, religious, or communal group. Mason, Wronski, & Kane's (2021) recent inquiry into a pronounced lack of bipartisanship in the US context investigated minority group support during the era of Donald Trump and found that social divisions, specifically, angst against minority groups was correlated with support for Trump. Along these lines, evidence has also been found for elite-based effects on democratic erosion, particularly through political rhetoric that incumbent leaders articulate during election cycles.

Davis et al. (2020) find support for a long stemming claim that many political analysts have observed throughout modern history – that elite rhetoric can undermine democratic norms. In their inquiry, Trump is once again the focal point and here, a multi-wave survey experiment is carried out in which exposure to the former President's Twitter activity and tweets are found to reduce trust and confidence in elections among his supporters. In contrast, Perello & Navia (2023) demonstrate how a different elite-based mechanism can come into play with regard to democratic backsliding. Through a case study of the National Party in Honduras, the authors reveal how incumbent governments used conditional cash transfers to upkeep electoral support while democratic institutions in the country backslid. A noticeable commonality in these aforementioned studies is decipherable. It appears that any form of democratic erosion or adversity to democratic norms is explained by either individual behavior(s), group-level problems, or elite-level rhetoric. Interestingly enough, key institutional processes, such as governments bailing out corporations during period of economic crisis or governments collaborating with tech conglomerates to either spy on civilians or amass swaths of data on civilian behavior are not considered as being evasive to democracy, at least in literature on backsliding.

Finally, it is important to consider that backsliding has also been attributed to global political shifts. Samuels (2023) argues that a potential source of backsliding around the world can be observed in the impact of reconfiguration of global politics after both the Cold War and 9/11. The contemporary international context provides fewer incentives for leaders to "stand up for democracy," in light of the rise of China and the role of both Chinese and Russian "meddling" in domestic politics in the United States. The key dynamic that Samuels contends has had (and continues to have) a causative effect on global patterns of democratic backsliding is the lack of incentives that the US possesses to defend liberal governance on a global scale combined with a lack of ideological content to international political competition – both factors were salient in the Cold War, but are "relatively weaker" today. In terms of 9/11, Samuels argues that it had a complimentary impact to the aforementioned dynamic – as foreign policy became driven by an "obsession with fighting terrorists," which in turn, undermined support for the global promotion of democracy and human rights.

Backsliding and the Pandemic?

It is unclear if democratic backsliding is actually a salient empirical phenomenon that has taken much of the world by storm in the last decade or if this literature comprises a trend of scholars selecting on their dependent variables and reaffirming one another's theoretical presuppositions. For a non-technical audience, selecting on the dependent variable means picking cases that either support one's theoretical or conceptual framework or inclinations, or picking cases in which researchers know a particular outcome did occur. Although there surely are a number of countries that have experienced democratic erosion, it might be the case that these countries attract the bulk of attention from social scientists, which in turn, conflates backsliding with a proposed trend of cross-national autocratization that may or may not actually be empirically factual.

Recent critical inquiry into these topics has revealed that measures of backsliding have been contingent on subjective interpretations of key variables and characteristics of democracy. At the time of writing this book, even with the incredible amount of attention that backsliding has received in scholarship and public discourse, there has not actually been a systematic inquiry that has tested whether this phenomenon has occurred on a global scale (Little & Meng, 2023). Little & Meng (2023) argue that we currently lack reliable ways to measure democracy and that historically, this has been a "notoriously hard problem" because scholars cannot agree on how democracy should be defined and what's more, specific components of it are difficult to code (Little & Meng, 2023, p. 2). The major issue in this increasingly prevalent literature, argue the authors, is that studies which have found evidence of global backsliding "rely heavily if not entirely on subjective indicators" (Little & Meng, 2023, p. 2). Specifically, of the current popularity attributed to V-Dem's democracy datasets, of V-Dem's five sub-indices, three (freedom of expression; association; clean elections) are demonstrated by the authors to be "entirely comprised of subjective expert-coded variables" (Little & Meng, 2023, p. 9).

As subsequent sections of this book will reveal, a major illiberal set of practices pertaining to surveillance capitalism are also not captured in formal measures of democracy. Moreover, Little & Meng's (2023) analysis of 20 different indicators of democratic performance demonstrated that if measures on democracy that are not beset by subjective coding interpretations are taken into consideration, democracies across the world are not actually performing worse in recent years and that democracy, on the whole, is largely stable.

It appears that the key variables and points of argumentation that tend to be emphasized in backsliding literature cannot account for pandemic responses in liberal democratic states, and specifically, the variance(s) that are inherent to these responses. For example, Sweden has long been hailed (and coded in democracy measures) as being within the top five of liberal democratic polities in the world and is a country that is generally observed to have not experienced backsliding in any significant form, yet its approach to the pandemic was far less restrictive than some of the common suspects of backsliders and populists (e.g., Poland or Hungary). Along similar lines, when incumbent governments that have been frequently classified as backsliders or populists (e.g., Brazil) took on lenient approaches to deal with the pandemic, their behavior was causally attributed to populism by scholars (Burni & Tamaki, 2021). Another issue in this literature can be observed in the largely US and Western European-centrist viewpoints that tend to pinpoint problems of democracy on American domestic phenomena such as polarization, ethnic cleavages, or elite-level antagonization and discourse. Here, the commonality of attributing agency to electoral cycles and processes tends to drive scholarly analyses and explanations, which in turn, miss out on other possible confounding factors. For example, an interesting point in Little & Meng's (2023) inquiry is that they find scholarly sentiment and attention on democratic backsliding increased beginning in 2016 – a year that was marked by the election of Donald Trump. The astonishing aspect here is noted by the authors as follows, "For instance, after the election of Donald Trump in 2016, Polity lowered the US's Polity2 score from 10 to 8, which is a lower score than the US during the Jim Crow era or prior to women's suffrage (Polity2 scores the US as a 9 during those periods)" (Little & Meng, 2023, p. 8). The United States' Polity2 score thus went from a 10 to an 8 after Trump was elected, then by 2020 it was lowered to 5 – a value that entails the country is no longer a full democracy and is on par with countries such as Somalia, Ecuador, Haiti, and Mozambique (Little & Meng, 2023, p. 8). The sheer subjective nature of these coding decisions reeks of political biases.

Glasius (2018) brings up a similar point in referring to the highly adverse (to human rights) American Central Intelligence Agency's rendition program which secretly detained, transported, and tortured political opponents and enemy combatants over the course of the G. W. Bush administration. Although few (if any at all) political scientists would classify the Bush administration as an authoritarian regime, just because this particular government was elected does not necessarily mean it cannot "merit the label of authoritarian," according to Glasius. Political science, argues Glasius, fails to offer clear answers to these important questions and topic as a whole (Glasius, 2018, p. 518).

Such approaches, as this book will demonstrate, only scrape at the surface of causal complexity that underlies the widely illiberal response that nearly all democracies took to deal with the pandemic. Just as other historical periods of crisis, the pandemic was exceedingly complex and driven by non-linear interactions of causal forces (Anisin, 2022d). What's more, these approaches also fail to account for key illiberal processes that arose during the pandemic throughout most liberal democratic states. The same can be said for populism, a literature which we will now turn to.

Populism and its Failure(s)

Although two different literatures, democratic backsliding and populism are often mentioned alongside one another. Populism has increasingly been associated with pandemic policies and outcomes. For example, Bustikova & Babos (2020) analyze populists in the Czech Republic and Slovakia during the height of the pandemic and argue that populist governments and political parties in these two countries exhibited erratic but technocratic policy making in which medical expertise was weaponized for political purposes. The article, like many in literature on populism, selects on the dependent variable by picking two countries and incumbent governments that fall under what the authors contend to be a sub-set of populism – technocratic populism (which differs from exclusionary populism and inclusionary populism) (Bustikova & Babos, 2020, p. 498). The article's main point of argumentation entails that technocratic populists politicize expertise and fool voters into giving their political support. During the pandemic in the two noted countries, technocratic populism led to expertise getting prioritized over deliberative debate (Bustikova & Babos, 2020, p. 501). The issue with this argument is not that the observed phenomena did not happen or that the authors' detailing of democratically adverse outcomes such as Czech Prime Minister Andrej Babis' sidestepping of the state's Central Emergency Task Force, but that there is no comparative component in the research design of the study. This makes the study narrow, conceptually, because without being able to observe similar outcomes (or their absence) in cases which similar policies were carried out, the causal nature of the phenomenon under attention is not able to be sufficiently unpacked. Specifically, we do not know if it was populism that was responsible for this type of coercive behavior on the part of the incumbent government or if other forces were responsible.

The adversities that were experienced throughout many liberal democratic states during the pandemic signify a deeper underlying set of tendencies which, can be accounted for by surveillance capitalism and its synthesis with authoritarian liberalism.

Introducing Authoritarian Liberalism

Authoritarian liberalism is a much less prominent academic framework when compared to populism and democratic backsliding. While it is tough to contemplate why this is so, a likely culprit is that academia is no less prone to fads than popular culture – each decade or so, new tendencies in the social world arise and to account for these tendencies, scholarly concepts get articulated and some concepts and frameworks catch on and gain steam (e.g., Fukuyama's End of History thesis or Huntington's Clash of Civilization). Over continuous reproduction, debate, and deliberation, some academic literatures contribute to paradigms of knowledge that dominate intellectual and public debates. Authoritarian liberalism is a concept that at the current point in time, still remains quite fringe in law and political theory and has not appeared in significant frequency either as a cited topic. This is especially observable across mainstream sociology and political science journals.

Authoritarian liberalism is premised on the classical liberal belief that a society should be based on competition and free market access but in conjunction, the role the state should play in the economy must not be infringed upon or hampered by democratic processes. The latter are assumed to potentially be able to prevent a given state from enforcing market efficiency and positive economic outcomes (Wilkinson, 2021, p. 27). The origins of authoritarian liberalism root back to the Weimar Republic in Germany and two particular theorists' ideas on the role of the state in the economy jurist Hermann Heller (2015 [1932]) and political and legal scholar Carl Schmitt. Both scholars' writings on state institutions and market functionality led to the articulation of a concept known as ordoliberalism which since has been either contrasted to or associated with authoritarian liberalism. Ordoliberalists emphasize that governments need to ensure fair market competition to produce beneficial outcomes across economic marketplaces. Authoritarian liberalism, in contrast, is premised on concentrating power to ensure market stability. Heller (2015) explained the emergence of authoritarian liberalism that he observed amongst his social order,

> The anti-democratic basis of the 'authoritarian' state is obvious. Far more difficult, but also far more revealing, is answering the question of the spheres of life in which the state is supposed to conduct itself in an authoritarian way and what limits its authority ought to respect according to the intentions of its spokesmen. It is precisely these limits of state authority that will turn out to be the true *experimentum crucis* of the 'authoritarian' state (Heller, 2015, p. 297).

Heller then argued that the potential success of a Völkisch national socialism is contingent on the belief that a culturally homogeneous population can brought about by "means of detour via an authoritarian economic community or an authoritarian racial community" (Heller, 2015, p. 298) – a statement that turned out to be quite an accurate projection of what the subsequent decade of Nazi-led Germany experienced. A commonality that was at play amongst advocates of authoritarian liberalism was that direct and mass democracy were detrimental to the Weimar Republic, and thus an authoritarian revival of the liberal state was obligatory to pursue. Along these lines, Schmitt believed that democracy ran risk of turning into "proletarian democracy" which could replace liberalism, and in turn, such fears bred ideological configurations that stressed the necessity of having a strong state with robust legal institutions. The latter would be engaged in reestablishing liberal economic market functionality when democracy became threatening to the liberal state's existence. Hence, the authoritarian liberal believes that representative democracy must be curtailed for the greater purpose of protecting economic liberalism and the value of respecting fiscal discipline (Kivotidis, 2021). Kivotidis (2021) makes an interesting (and in my view, accurate) set of claims by noting that authoritarian liberalism signifies a current form of bourgeois class dictatorship and likewise it signifies a historical trajectory in which democratic states have undergone transformations.

Although Kivotidis' argument preceded the pandemic, it is important to consider as here it is noted that authoritarian liberalism sought to "insulate decision-making processes from popular strata" and to restrict access in decision making (Kivitodis, 2021, p. 111). The current authoritarian liberal structure of the EU is thus not a design fault, but is driven by a logic of bourgeois class dictatorship that views democracy as an impediment to achieving a free labor economy (Kivitodis, 2021, p. 112).

Wilkinson's (2021) work puts forward similar claims. Along these lines, readers may perceive that the distinction between authoritarian liberalism is not conceptually clear or different from neoliberalism. Hence, it is vital to point out that these phenomena are unalike. Neoliberalism arose along with Thatcher and Reagan at the height of Western deindustrialization. Neoliberalism is much newer, historically, than authoritarian liberalism. It is also quite a different framework because it is necessary anti-state and anti-regulation in its caricature. In contrast, authoritarian liberalism constitutes processes that have arisen over the course of the twentieth and twenty-first centuries in which states have merged with markets during periods of crisis and contingency to spur "efficient" outcomes – such policies have importantly functioned through illiberal practices and have adversely impacted entire populations apart from economic and political elites.

Importantly, the origin of authoritarian liberalism is in a right-wing response to democratic processes that arose during the Weimar Republic. Authoritarian liberalism was articulated as a critique of democracy to protect democracy from communist forces. By the 1950s authoritarian liberalism adjoined the idea that mass democracy leads to "unfreedom" argues Bonefeld (2017). The 1970s experienced salient crises that stemmed to the global supply of oil, the creation of credit systems, and the end of Keynesian monetary policies. Authoritarian liberalism necessarily features usage of authoritarian behavior and actions that are waged to uphold capitalist structures through supporting the liberal state, laws, private property, and associated concentrated forms of power. Already as early as the 1930s, attempts to restrict democracy in the name of defending democracy from communist threats led to a successful depoliticization of the liberal economy. Liberal politics became the only form of acceptable governance for a state to pursue. Alongside these components, authoritarian liberals then markedly restricted and successfully prevented the formation of collective labor demands by convincing masses that a free-market economy is equivalent to freedom and that it "amounts to a practice of government" (Bonefeld, 2017, p. 4). In pursuing these motivations and policies, authoritarian liberals drew upon technological means and military technology to make sure citizens were carrying out "rightful conduct" (Bonefeld, 2017, p. 6).

Next, a few words must also be said about Wilkinson's (2021) comparison of authoritarian liberalism to neoliberalism. In his monograph on authoritarian liberalism, Wilkinson notes that even though it is not uncommon to consider neoliberalism as an authoritarian phenomenon, authoritarian liberalism stands in contrast to democratic governance because it sets it aside. Neoliberalism however, is not necessarily anti-democratic, even if its outcomes are indeed disadvantageous to the general standing of democracy due to creating inequality and dampening prospects of class struggle. Over the last several decades, authoritarian liberalist policies have successfully turned social democratic politics away from working-class communities in favor of the "domination of policymaking by liberal-techno-cratic elites" (Wilkinson, 2021, p. 282).

The pandemic, as subsequent empirical analyses will demonstrate, nurtured a new fusion between policy makers and liberal-technocratic elites across different spheres of governmentality.

Surveillance Capitalism

The phenomenon of surveillance capitalism constitutes arguably the most salient change in socio-political conditions that has arisen in the 21st century thus far. This phenomenon, unfortunately, is not theorized, measured, nor incorporated into formal measures of democracy in aforementioned literature on democratic backsliding and populism. Zuboff (2019) contends that surveillance capitalism triggered a massive change in socio-political affairs because it is an "antidemocratic and anti-egalitarian juggernaut" that arose through numerous trajectories of corporate dominance that are resemblant of a "market-driven coup from above" (Zuboff, 2019, p. 513). Some would probably go so far as to argue that this phenomenon has fundamentally transformed the nature of our relation to economic markets. In terms of historical precedent and potential comparisons of similar transmutations in human history, the transition from an agricultural and agrarian society to an urban industrial society was probably the last time that such profound changes in history can be observed. While it is indeed true that the discovery of bacteria, the subsequent advent of modern medicine, and the development of vaccines did lead to improvements in life expectancy and a global population boom, surveillance capitalism's impact is so profound that none of us have encountered or seen such a fundamental change in human relations in our lifetimes.

Zuboff (2019) describes the central characteristics of surveillance capitalism as follows,

[1.] hidden commercial practices of extraction, prediction, and sales; 2. A parasitic economic logic in which the production of goods and services is subordinated to a new global architecture of behavioral modification; 3. A rogue mutation of capitalism marked by concentrations of wealth, knowledge, and power unprecedented in human history; 4. The foundational framework of a surveillance economy; 5. As significant a threat to human nature in the twenty-first century as industrial capitalism was to the natural world in the nineteenth and twentieth; 6. The origin of a new instrumentarian power that asserts dominance over society and presents startling challenges to market democracy; 7. A movement that aims to impose a new collective order based on total certainty; 8. An expropriation of critical human rights that is best understood as a coup from above: an overthrow of the people's sovereignty (Zuboff, 2019, vii).

Zuboff's categorization of this phenomenon is multi-dimensional because surveillance capitalism features several technological components such as artificial intelligence (and associated mechanisms of deep learning and machine learning); individual-based usage and behaviors with technological tools (mobile phones, computers, smartwatches, etc.), and engagement with online eco-systems and networks. In addition, Zuboff places emphasis on the different trajectories that tech companies have taken to dictate and modify human behavior through their monopolies over human knowledge in the digital sphere. Writing in *the Socio-Economic Review,* Fourcade & Healy (2017) argue that information dragnets yield large quantities of individual-level data that are used to deepen the reach of the market and foster new strategies for profit making. Profit is based on individuals' data, which they voluntarily succumb to giving tech corporations every time they use or sign up for a given app or service. Building off of Zuboff's intuition, the authors show how modern organizations follow institutional data imperatives to collect as much data as possible and then to spur capital flows through digital scoring and ranking methodologies.

This all takes place in an alternative or digital reality that subsides alongside our normal reality – human beings across much of the developed world are entrenched in internet-based forms of communication which are increasingly supplanting and taking up more of our time. People spend swaths of their working days and free time on internet-based forms of technology wherein they communicate with family, friends, loved ones, members of their community, and with other people from near and far. All of our information, habitual practices, preferences, shopping history, and communicational patterns are stored in corporate surveillance structures. Digital forms of technology are now utilized by individuals for the most basic of services such as paying one's bills, shopping for food, dating, funeral planning, vacation planning, schooling, and entertainment. In shifting from largely in-person to digital based communication and social practices, we have succumbed to providing our data and personal information to companies and governments, often with little reflection on the implications that this may pose for our own personal interests, wellbeing, and collective involvement. Unfortunately, the pandemic plunged humanity even deeper into reliance on digital forms of communication and technological based social behavior.

All of these new tendencies associated with surveillance capitalism are not random, but were made possible by the emergence of internet-based technologies that were developed and made available to consumers. Zuboff (2019) demonstrated how there now exists a proprietorship pattern of a new means of production – information. For most people that live in the "developed world" the demarcation between virtual and non-virtual reality is either blurred or nonexistent. Statistical tendencies on how much individuals spend on screen time, computer and smartphone usage, and digital communication speak for themselves. Similar to how identities rapidly changed as a result of millions of peasants being forced from their land during economic dislocations that led to a reshaping of economies and practices during the 17th, 18th and 19th centuries, the shift from a service economy to a surveillance capitalistic economy has had profound impacts on all facets of our lives. These impacts however, have not been adequately theorized in measures of democracy, nor in academic scholarship on democratic backsliding and populism.

Baker, & Huang's (2023) inquiry offers a glimpse into these transformative dynamics. In recent years, data breaches of technological corporations have revealed that they have massive stores of data on human behavior, most of which individuals have no idea they are "giving" to a application or platform when agreeing to install and use it on their smartphone. In a different reading of surveillance capitalism, Venkatesh (2021) adopts a Marxian perspective to argue that Marx's categorization of industrial capitalists versus workers closely resembles contemporary relationships between surveillance capitalists and users of digital platforms and consumers. The Marxian concepts of accumulation, alienation, and exploitation are argued by the author to be heavily present across surveillance capitalistic societies. In contrast to Zuboff however, Venkatesh argues that the nature of exchanges that take place between surveillance capitalists and users is voluntary, while Zuboff believes it to be a form of raw material gathering or theft. It might be the case that both of these dynamics are prevalent at different points in time and according to the specific company or process under attention. Prior to the pandemic, there was a voluntary nature inherent to how individuals would give up their information to a given service or application – if someone does not want their data getting hoarded by a given tech company, they simply cannot use the said service. However, during the pandemic, such information was literally treated as raw material that was handed over to state security institutions by technological and telecommunication corporations who provided governments with data architecture to surveillance and place entire populations on lockdowns – lockdowns that hitherto had never been experienced or initiated to such a large and temporally elongated extent.

Garrett's (2022) inquiry on surveillance capitalism during the pandemic is one of the few that have been produced to date in which these topics are both linked. Garrett's analysis is carried out through the guise of social work and here it is argued that new forms of surveillance will become socially embedded due to crises associated with the pandemic. The study highlights the anti-democratic nature of surveillance capitalism and points to the lack of public debate that accompanied "magic bullet" responses that were used to tackle the virus by public health officials through surveillance technology. Garrett (2022) draws upon the examples of Poland (where smartphones were literally used to quarantine people) and facial recognition and biometric identification technologies that are being developed in the United Kingdom (e.g., the NHSX). In the US, smartphone-based data tracking of civilians was engineered through a data mining company called Palantir which was funded by a CIA venture capital fund (Garrett, 2022, p. 1758). There are many more examples of similar type that can be observed to have arisen across liberal democratic polities. The fourth and sixth chapters of this book will delve deep into how different technologies were developed then enforced (with lack of deliberative debate and little parliamentary overview) across nearly all waves of the pandemic and in nearly all countries in the sample under attention.

Treguer's (2021) inquiry offered a preliminary look into the impact that the health crisis brought about by COVID-19 could have on digital state surveillance. Here it was argued that state surveillance during epidemics can be accounted for by Foucault's concept of "regimes of power" through analysis of surveillance practices in Italy, France, the US and the UK. Regimes of power foster public-private assemblages in which health data are managed and then justified by policy makers. Justification itself is a form of legitimization and is accomplished in the backdrop of health emergencies. Similarly, Bibri & Allam (2022) investigate the Metaverse which they describe as a "gigantic ecosystem application enabled mainly by Artificial Intelligence (AI), the IoT, Big Data, and Extended Reality (XR) technologies" – constituting a "parallel virtual environment" that is run by the conglomerate, Facebook. Interestingly enough, Facebook launched the Metaverse project during the pandemic because the crisis was a rare opportunity that the corporation thought should be seized "to reset and reimaging the world" through digital "reincarnation" (Bibri & Allam, 2022). The authors reveal how the Metaverse has already set social status quos in which living in a "new normal" virtual environment has become not only accepted by masses, but applauded by them. Metaverse's dominance arose through processes that led to the normalization of a corporate-led top-down algorithmic mode of governance that has successfully established control over living in urban societies.

The pandemic fostered a new synthesis between authoritarian liberalism and surveillance capitalism. To understand why this occurred, we must contextualize antecedent conditions. This global health crisis arose in a time that was marked by the digitalization of social reality and the presence of what Zuboff (2019) accurately describes to be a palpable imbalance between the accumulation and possession of information and surveillance capitalists' access to our "private" or personal data. As subsequent chapters of this book will reveal, the pandemic led to international liberal institutions (i. e., the World Health Organization), regional institutions (e. g., the European Commission), and incumbent governments (who head national economies and polities) to carry out the largest project of surveillance of populaces in liberal democratic history. This project accompanied the most significant and severe forms of restrictions on human movement, economic activity, schooling, social interactions, and the tracing of public health parameters in history. These outcomes could not have been made possible without the antecedent presence of surveillance capitalism and the conditions that it instilled throughout societies, but at the same time, surveillance capitalism on its own cannot explain all adverse phenomena that arose throughout the pandemic without theoretical aid of authoritarian liberalism. The synthesis between these two frameworks and their empirical manifestation represents a radical departure from all previous eras of liberal democratic history.

Chapter 3: Theoretical Framework and Research Design

Introduction

This chapter will theorize both how and why democratically adverse outcomes arose during the pandemic through connecting the framework of authoritarian liberalism to surveillance capitalism. In several preliminary inquiries that I carried out on pandemic restrictions within the EU context, I identified mechanisms that were operative throughout different causal processes that led to outcomes that were averse to the standing and status of liberal democracy. Since this book analyzes a large sample of country level cases (n=54), the form that my theorization will take in the following paragraphs is meant to be moderately general because these claims are applied to countries that are heterogeneous. This chapter will also delve deep into different periods of crises that have arisen across the 20th century and thus far in the 21st century through the prism of authoritarian liberalism. Where necessary, I will also draw from the framework of surveillance capitalism and then theorize how both frameworks constitute a powerful explanatory pretext that can account for numerous adverse outcomes that arose during the pandemic over the course of 2020–22.

More than three years removed from the onset of the pandemic, it is clear that COVID-19 led to a plethora of different disruptions of status quos, many of which were responded with by governments through enacting states of emergencies. In legal and political science scholarship, the concept of "emergency politics" (Wolkenstein, 2021) has been used to account for unconventional or extreme measures which can arise during political instability, terrorism threats, and even a pandemic. Often, crises constitute temporal periods of time in which political power is exercised and antecedent phenomena that were lurking and active in the background come into fruition. Crises also constitute dislocations to social structures and during periods of dislocation, actors and elites articulate different political ideas, symbols, and ideological configurations to make sense of the contingent nature of social and historical reality (Laclau, 1990).

To understand the underlying characteristics of illiberal outcomes that arose throughout the pandemic, previous empirical phenomena relating to authoritarian liberalism and surveillance capitalism must be considered and theorized. This chapter will demonstrate that a given phenomenon such as authoritarian liberalism can indeed change in its parameters and manifest in different ways as time goes on, but importantly, during such changes, the phenomenon evolves and accli-

https://doi.org/10.1515/9783111345703-003

matizes itself according to crises that arise. During the pandemic, previously sedi-
mented authoritarian liberal policies merged with surveillance capitalistic processes to bring about the most significant and wide-reaching restrictions on civil liberties in liberal democratic history. Throughout this turbulent period of recent
history, democratic norms and values were sidestepped in favor of corporate interests. Most liberal democratic states took on authoritarian liberal responses to the
pandemic and surveillance capitalistic structures were widely drawn upon in attempt to regulate and optimize human beings' biological parameters.

Differentiating Authoritarian Liberalism from Backsliding and Populism

Instead of the commonly identified factor of deception that is mentioned in research on populism, authoritarian liberalism is not contingent on one politician,
government, or set of political actors. Elites and governing parties are not necessarily deceiving but rather, they take on measures and pass policies that are favor-
able to corporate and large-scale economic interests. These measures have repeatedly been accomplished through illiberal practices and have historically been
implemented at the expense and interests of working and middle classes. Authoritarian liberals have an interest in depoliticizing masses from offsetting the formation of politically and economically threatening demands.

Authoritarian liberalism is, in multiple ways, a complicated concept because it
does not contradict the fundamental basis of liberalism – political and economic
elites that engage in authoritarian liberal practices do not strip private property
away from civilians, do not nationalize industries, and may not even tamper
with or rig election cycles or shut down independent media outlets. Instead, a government carries out decision making and replaces parliament as a key state institution, and while doing so, it takes on several tasks such as liberating the economy,
depoliticizing socio-economic relations, and making sure labor power remains at a
level that is high enough for the economy to function (Bonefeld, 2017).

Authoritarian liberal elites have asserted themselves as "the concentrated
force of a depoliticized exchange society in which the individuals compete and exchange with one another as owners of private property, the one buying labour
power, the other selling it in freedom from coercion and as equals in the eye of
the law" (Bonefeld, 2017, p. 3). If one of the fundamental premises of democracy
is that elected officials have to appeal to and serve the preferences of the median
voter, then periods of economic crisis over the last near century of history have
demonstrated how authoritarian liberalism has subverted democracy and in
doing so, authoritarian liberals have undermined the interests of the median

voter. As noted by Bonefeld (2017), authoritarian liberalism entails that "freedom needs to be protected against the enemies of freedom even if they move formally within the legal bounds of a free society and secure parliamentary majorities by free elections" (Bondfeld, 2017, p. 3).

Bonefeld (2017) also reasons that authoritarian liberalism is premised by the vision of an economy that is self-sufficient and an economy that subsides alongside a "state-less sphere" in which demands and citizen preferences are by and large depoliticized. The latter is a crucial dynamic for readers to associate with the nature of authoritarian liberalism because during periods of socio-economic or socio-political ruptures, this is precisely what can keep populational demands from amassing into a threatening social movement.

Furthermore, as noted by Bonefeld, "the achievement of a 'state-less' economic sphere amounts fundamentally to a political task. It is instituted and enforced by the state, and it is also supervised by the state to secure and sustain the rule-based conduct of the free entrepreneurs of labour power" (Bonefeld, 2017, p. 9). Since the early 1980s, a plethora of new economic crises and examples of authoritarian liberal practices can be observed. These include behaviors and policies of the European Union in which monopoly holders (states) implement rules that get decided by European supranational institutions; the provisioning of billions of dollars (or euros) to bailout corporations in time of economic crises; the restructuring of states' failed economies, among many other assorted outcomes that force populations under what Bonefeld plausibly categorizes as a "regime of imposed liberty" (Bonefeld, 2017, p. 11).

Up until the pandemic, no better example of these dynamics could be observed than in the 2007–8 global financial crisis and its aftermath in the 2011 Eurozone crisis. In 2007–8, a massive economic recession arose when the average prices of homes in the United States began to dramatically fall. This led to several of the world's biggest banks (Lehman Brothers) to file for bankruptcy. Underpinning this downward economic trajectory were ill-practices associated with government-led incentives that were handed off to banks to encourage unqualified consumers to take out loans on properties and houses. In conjunction, the crisis was also driven by insider trading in which hedge funds and trading firms adversely exchanged information and dealt their investments in aforementioned subprime loans. This led to trillions of US dollars left hanging in mortgage investments valueless. Global repercussions were incredible – the world economy experienced an estimated 3.8% drop (Figus & de Serio, 2021). The US economy experienced a near 5% drop, while the Eurozone experienced just over 5%.

Rather than letting big corporations and banking structures "fail" according to market forces, central governments and incumbent political leaders engaged in the biggest bailouts of large-scale industry and corporations that the world had seen to date. The first of these packages gave hundreds of billions of dollars (442 billion to be precise) to Freddie Mac and Fannie Mae – both of which are enterprises of the Federal National Mortgage Association. These institutions and their associated organs were bailed out at the expensive of the tax payer and working and middle classes. Bankers were not the only corporate actors that got bailed out by the Federal government, as corporations from the auto industry also were bailed out. More on these dynamics is said in chapter six of this book.

By 2011, different parts of the world began to experience turmoil due to downstream effects of 2007– 8 crisis, including much of the Middle East and Southern Europe. This led to both attempted and successful revolutions during the Arab Spring and a massive socio-economic crisis and subsequent bailouts in places such as Greece, Cyprus, Spain, and Portugal. The Eurozone crisis as it came to be known, was an extension of what Wilkinson argues was an earlier reconstitution of Europe that occurred in the post-war and Maastricht eras. This laid the grounds for the responses that arose during the Eurozone crisis. In addition, the 1997 Treaty of Amsterdam along with the Schengen system helped to open the door to differentiated integration that marked "a change in the material and ideological balance of power" – wherein any existing alternative to hegemonic neo-liberalism and liberal capitalism was eradicated (Wilkinson, 2021, p. 205). The 2011 Eurozone crisis also marked a long process of depoliticization, argues Wilkinson, as "European integration reinforced the edifice of authoritarian liberalism through its institutional procedures of consensual law- making, constitutionalization of the Treaty provisions, and entrenched commitments to market liberalism and technocratic authority" (Wilkinson, 2021, p. 205 – 6). Member states were thus left with a complete absence of channels to challenge or contest the EU political processes, which in turn, led to an adverse dynamic in which the "Only option was to politically contest Europe itself" (Wilkinson, 2021, p. 206). Through coercive fashion, "elected heads of governments would be dispatched and replaced with technocratic leaders, notably in Italy and Greece" (Wilkinson, 2021, p. 206). These developments were carried out under the guises of necessity and emergency, and in the process, deliberative supranationalism was forgotten (Wilkinson, 2021, p. 206). Subsequent chapters of this book will reveal how COVID-19 policies across liberal democracies were all (nearly) carried out under emergency decrees and through similar guises of necessity.

Before getting to the critical juncture of my theoretical framework, a few words must be said about events that arose at the time of writing this book. In Spring of 2023, another economic crisis was looming when downturn ensued after several large American banks (Silicon Valley Bank, SVB) declared bankruptcy due to adverse processes that were carried out in response to the Federal Reserve's interest rate hikes. To try to beat out the adverse impacts that interest rates had on the financial equity of banks, numerous banks (such as SVB) invested out of government bonds and put money into more murkier areas at a lower interest rate. And again, similar to 2007–8 and Bernard Madoff's massive securities fraud of an estimated $64 Billion, high ranking bankers and wealthy individuals of SVB sold their shares prior to their bank's collapse. For instance, the CEO of SVB (Greg Becker) and the CFO (Daniel Beck) sold significant portions of their shares prior to the collapse. These individuals (and others) are being sued by investors (Hrushka, 2023).

After the downturn of SVB, the following banks also experienced near collapse: Silvergate; Signature Bank; First Republic; Credit Suisse; Deutsche Bank, among others. Analogous to the 2007–8 crises, the Federal government stepped in, once again, and implemented a large-scale package that sought to prevent a larger domino-effect. In March 2023, the Federal Reserve pumped an estimated $33 Billion into the banking sector and took over SVB. As noted by Stewart (2023), early on in the SVB crisis, taxpayer money would reportedly not be drawn on to bailout banks (or to return customers' deposits and account funds) as was the case during the bailouts of 2008 because the government would draw from the Deposit Insurance Fund which is a private institution that provides up to $250,000 in insurance money to individuals or organizations. The fund is supported by the Federal Deposit Insurance Corporation (FDIC) which is reliant on treasury securities that are described by many as instruments of government debt.

Aforementioned banks that are based in the US all were allowed to borrow what Helmore (2023) described as "essentially unlimited amounts from the Federal Reserve for the next year, as long as the loans are matched by safe government securities, a way to prevent financial firms from having to sell a class of investments that have been losing value because of the Fed's own high interest rate policies" (Helmore, 2023). As experienced in the 2000s, during the pandemic, and in 2023, more and more money was printed, inflation increased while the national debt piled on with no end in sight.

Authoritarian Liberalism, Censorship, and Surveillance Capitalism

The pandemic fostered a new synthesis between authoritarian liberalism and surveillance capitalism – particularly through the former's utilization of the latter's ability to censor and depoliticize the public. Very recent information that made it into mainstream news waves at the tail end of the pandemic reveals the extent to which surveillance capitalism has become embedded into state security institutions. At the time of writing this book, several US journalists revealed the "Twitter

Files" which arose as a part of Elon Musk's reformation of Twitter and the company's long stemming blocking and de-platforming policies. The Twitter Files constitute arguably the largest leaked set of documents on government-led surveillance since E. Snowden's whistleblowing leaks back in 2013. Snowden provided evidence that government security agencies (the National Security Agency, NSA) were widely spying on American citizens without warrants and with aid of private telecommunication corporations' infrastructure, data, and resources. The conglomerate, AT&T, engaged in a "highly collaborative" relationship with the NSA and gave access to billions of emails that flowed across its networks domestically in the US through internet communications (Angwin et al., 2015).

A report from 2015 indicated that there were at least 17 different surveillance hubs that functioned through AT&T and their functionality dated back to the post 9/11 era. By 2011, the corporation handed over 1.1 billion domestic cellphone calling records a day to the NSA (Angwin et al., 2015). As readers that are familiar with these revelations will acknowledge, there is obviously much more to this complex story and state security institutions' collaboration with private companies have been discovered to not only be an American phenomenon, but other historical beacons of liberal democracy, such as the United Kingdom, engaged in similar practices. For example, a 2014 BBC report (which at the time, was a part of a long array of British media output) revealed that the British spy agency (Government Communications Headquarters, GCHQ) also tapped fiber-optic cables as a part of a massive data collection effort in which up to 600 million communicational exchanges from private individuals were analyzed per day (BBC News, 2014). At the height of his whistleblowing activities, Snowden did an interview with the British press outlet, The Guardian, and revealed that, "It's not just a US problem. The UK has a huge dog in this fight," Snowden told the Guardian. "They [GCHQ] are worse than the US" (MacAskill et al., 2013).

In contrast to the NSA and GCHQ's activities, the Twitter Files reveal that a much more targeted set of efforts were carried out over the course of the Trump administration's time in office, throughout the height of the pandemic, and into the first years of the Biden administration's incumbency. According to Shellenberger (2023), the Twitter Files show how state attorney general lawsuits and investigative reporting led to previously censored practices and information on networks of government agencies, academic institutions, and private groups that censored American citizens without their knowledge on topics that include the origin of COVID-19, vaccinations, and an array of other issues associated with the pandemic (Shellenberger, 2023). This occurred through a complex arrangement of censorship mechanisms, with the most significant being the FBI's entrenchment into the Twitter managerial hierarchy at different points in time during the 2019–20 election and the first year of the pandemic. The legal basis of these infiltrations into censoring masses of people's online behavior is in Section 2030 of the Telecommunications Decency Act of 1996 – a piece of legislation that attempts to regulate third-party data and has become one of the most controversial acts in recent US history. The Twitter files reveal how state security institutions have repeatedly demanded that social media companies censor or de-platform particular ideas, accounts, and trending topics that are deemed threatening to socio-political status quos or accounts that were considered to have engaged in "inauthentic behavior" across an estimated 40,000 Twitter profiles (Kumar, 2023).

There is a key latent dynamic that likely played a role in these censorship processes. This dynamic is quite technical but very important in terms of the effects it likely has on actual censorship outcomes. Algorithmic censorship is when either endogenous (actors within a social media company) or exogenous (actors from state security institutions) request that specific content get removed (but not erased or taken down) from social media trending topics lists. This is a covert form of censorship that is very complimentary to the authoritarian liberal's playbook – it does not disable liberal institutions (i.e., independent media companies) from existing or functioning, but rather, it depoliticizes their content and outputs, which in turn, can easily impact public opinion. Many democracy measures and datasets that are used in social science (and specifically, in literature on democratic backsliding and populism) as chapter five of this book will demonstrate, are not apt to capture these latent and clandestine dynamics in their measurement and coding schemes.

Furthermore, Shellenberger (2023) argues that, "in a few short years, federal government officials, agencies and contractors have gone from fighting ISIS recruiters and Russian bots to censoring and de-platforming ordinary Americans and disfavored public figures" (Shellenberger, 2023). The Twitter files and associated news stories made into congressional hearings in late 2022 an early 2023. They have been considered by elected officials and by established taskforces throughout different inquiries and probes which were launched into possible malpractices and constitutionally illegal behaviors. For example, on March 9, 2023, a House Judiciary Select Subcommittee carried out a hearing and examination on the Twitter Files in which Shellenberger and another journalist, Matt Taibi, were orally questioned. The hearing established that Twitter did indeed take down information at the request of exogenous actors and that in doing so, the company justified its censorship and removal of content by arguing that these pieces of news were a part of a "Russian disinformation" campaign. Similar exchanges were made with reference to Anthony Fauci and pandemic "misinformation."

In 2023, the former director of the Center for Disease Control and Prevention (CDC), Dr. Robert Redfield (who was in charge of the CDC during 2020) testified to Congress that Anthony Fauci excluded and removed him from policy discussions because of his views, which were at the time, against the dominant narrative that was floating around on the origin of the virus being from a food market in the province of Wuhan, China. Similar dynamics arose on a much larger scale when government officials successfully ended up censoring numerous scientific debate points surrounding the origin of COVID-19 and vaccination across social media platforms. This led to a pending lawsuit in two high profile cases – Missouri v. Biden and Hoeg v. Newsome, both of which allege that the Great Barrington Declaration (which was put forward in October 2020) enabled the Federal government to coerce social media corporations into censoring alternative viewpoints on COVID-19 policies (through algorithmic manipulation and deplatforming) under the pretext of "misinformation" or "disinformation" – policies which the plaintiffs argue violate both First and Fourteenth Amendment Rights. Similar topics were heard in the European Parliament in Spring of 2023 surrounding the pandemic, censorship, and pharmaceutical corporations' profiteering during the European Parliament's International COVID Summit III (Ateba, 2023). While these are clearly still cases that are going through investigative procedures, it is of importance to acknowledge that across liberal democracies, from the US to Canada, to Europe to Australia, a multitude of different forms of surveillance arose during the pandemic.

Theoretical Assumptions

First, in liberal democracies, mass state-led surveillance of populations during the pandemic could not have been possible without collaboration, cooperation, and direct involvement of private telecommunication and technology companies. Specifically, these companies' data on private individuals' behavior, consumption patterns, communication, and geolocation histories (and capability of geolocation-based tracking) were necessary for states to carry out the largest systematic surveillance project in their history. The synthesis of authoritarian liberalism with surveillance capitalism was conditional on the behavior and actions of state actors and political elites, economic elites (surveillance capitalists), and the antecedent amassing of data. A particular condition that readers should pay attention to here pertains to the accumulation of data that private technological corporations and companies have enjoyed through the rise of surveillance capitalism over the last two decades. The data and the technologies that surveillance capitalists (and their company's employees) utilize to gather and analyze are sophisticated and require a great amount of analytical and programming knowledge to decipher – so much that it is plausible to assume that state security institutions not only needed the data that private companies held of their civilian customers, but that they also needed the analytical know-how possessed by surveillance capitalists. I hypothesize that empirically, the synthesis between surveillance capitalism and authoritarian liberalism in the sphere of surveillance manifested through the forging of new connections between security institutions and private telecommunication and technology companies.

Second, authoritarian liberalism's manifestation during the pandemic was reliant on spurring outcomes that were pro-market, but only for particular types of organized economic interests. By organized economic interests, I refer to corporate interests which were prioritized and favored by governing political elites at the expensive of organized labor and small to medium sized businesses and their associated welfares. This was specifically done through the enforcement of economic and social restrictions which ended up arising in some segments of the economic marketplace and society, but not in others. Here, it is important to acknowledge that the first and second waves of the pandemic caused a massive drop in GDP in most liberal democracies, especially those in the Northern Hemisphere. For example, the US experienced a 32.9% drop in the second quarter of 2020 which was the one of the worst drops in its history (Horsley, 2020). If observed from 2019–2021, the US economy contracted at a rate which is estimated to constitute the worst recession ever (Mutikani, 2021). On a global scale, the entire world economy in 2020 shrunk by an estimated rate of 3.4%, amounting to more than two trillion dollars of lost productivity. During these turbulent waves of the pandemic, authoritarian liberal policies favored large scale economic enterprises, especially in the spheres of household consumption. Additionally, other conglomerates were allowed to operate and keep their doors open, while small to medium sized businesses were forced to shut. The key aspect about these restrictions and shutdowns is that they were enforced through immense aid of digital means and via digital surveillance – both of which would not have been possible in absence of an antecedent surveillance capitalistic configurations.

Third, policy makers and ministries of health sought to not only prevent the virus from spreading, but sought to "optimize" workforces through controlling and monitoring their bodily functionality (and dysfunctionality) via digital health parameter data structures. These processes saw the diffusion of health policies from international health institutions, primarily the WHO, which recommended and put out policy messages that were then adopted by supra-regional and regional organizations and then by incumbent governments in most countries in the sample of cases analyzed throughout this book. In pursuing record levels of profit, pharmaceutical corporations produced vaccines which were then exported throughout much of the world. The key aspect to pharmaceutical corporations' incentives to profiteer from the pandemic was not limited to "natural" forces of the economic marketplace, as authoritarian liberal political elites joined in to make policies that would disable global market competition from other countries' vaccines. Pfizer experienced a 1.82% increase in profit in 2020, but by 2021, it saw a 95.16% increase in profit ($81.28 billion), which led to another 23.43% increase for 2022. By 2022, Pfizer experienced a record $100 billion in profit, more than half of which was driven by its vaccine and COVID-19 antiviral treatment pills (Kimball, 2023).

Upon close examination, there are clear authoritarian liberal characteristics at play here. Specifically, vaccines created in the US and Britain, (e. g., Johnson & Johnson, Pfizer or Oxford-AstraZeneca) were promoted and heavily propagated while those produced in China (Sinoharm, Sinovac, and CanSino Biologics) and Russia (Sputnik V) were literally banned in nearly the entire Western part of the world and what's more, civilian travelers who had been vaccinated with either of these vaccines were not permitted to enter many Western (and pro-Western) countries. By mid-2021, only four vaccines were approved by the European Medicines Agency and these (expectedly) included Comirnaty (BioNTech, Pfizer), COVID-19 Vaccine Moderna, Vaxzevria (previously COVID-19 Vaccine AstraZeneca), and COVID-19 Vaccine Janssen (Johnson & Johnson) (Schengen Visa, 2021). These vaccines, as the subsequent chapter of this book will reveal, dictated individuals' travel ability and were at the heart of vaccine passport-based travel, QR Codes, and cross-border movement policies. The anti-Eastern produced vaccine consensus was not scientific nor premised on any sound medical research. By February of 2021, *The Lancet*, put out a report that indicated the Sputnik V vaccine's efficiency rate was 91.6% and did not produce any adverse side effects (Wishnick, 2021). Similar results have been found pertaining to vaccines produced by the Chinese state.

At the time of writing this book, China arguably features the most widespread and technologically developed system of social surveillance in the history of the nation state system and it is of immense important to demarcate this wide-reaching system from those that have been implemented in liberal democracies during the pandemic. I am not arguing that liberal democracies utilized the same extent of surveillance during the pandemic as the Chinese did prior, during, or after the pandemic. The types of surveillance that were implemented throughout most liberal democratic contexts nevertheless were based upon a syntheses of surveillance capitalism and authoritarian liberalism – this synthesis had much more in common with the Chinese approach to COVID-19 than many care to acknowledge. One of Anthony Fauci's main deputies, Dr. Clifford Lane, stated that he was "very impressed" with China's management of the pandemic in 2020 (Children's Health Defense Fund, 2022). With this being said, the synthesis between authoritarian liberalism and surveillance capitalism must be made distinct from what has been ongoing in China – as the Chinese state has had total control over communicational flows and digital information since the onset of the digital age. Liberal democracies have tended to experience quite a different trajectory of development in which private technological companies arose through capitalistic markets to then attract large swaths of customers who would use platforms for communication and social interactions. It was only after a certain amount of time went by that state security institutions began to infiltrate into corporate communicational structures – the pandemic, as subsequent chapters will reveal, intensified these processes.

Research Design

The methodological approaches adopted throughout this book will begin with a temporally sensitive analysis of each of the five waves of the pandemic in the subsequent chapter (chapter four). This analysis will be based on documents, policy reports, news media articles, scientific and peer reviewed studies as well as other accompanying information such as court hearings, trials, and information on the pandemic that is publicly available. The analysis is chronological and begins in the first month of 2020 then shifts into the different waves of the pandemic. As waves one, two, and three were by far the most lethal, the highest frequency of restrictions were carried out by governments and supranational institutions during this time. My classification of pandemic waves is based on epidemiological observations drawn from Amin et al. (2022) who identified five consecutive epidemiological waves of COVID-19 with the origin of the pandemic being observed in December of 2019 in China. Through analysis of epidemiological data from Tehran, Iran, the authors categorize following time periods – January-April 2020 (Wave 1); April 2020 – November 2020 (Wave 2); November 2020 – May 2021 (Wave 3); May 2021 – September 2021 (Wave 4); September 2021 – December 2021 (Wave 5).

Information on the consecutive waves of the pandemic was accessed in a manner that enabled me to account for stories, opinions, analyses, and news of events that arose in each wave. Some of the information that was made available at the height of the pandemic (the year 2020 and the beginning part of 2021) was later interpreted in different ways and in some instances, revealed to be quite different than was originally understood. Moreover, I drew upon the World Health Organization and its formal statements and policy reports. Where necessary, I drew upon data from other institutional bodies that are domestic such as the Center for Disease and Control and each country's (in the sample) respective government health institution.

Investigating the theoretical claims that were put forward in the previous chapter of this book are going to first be done through empirical analysis of processes that arose during different waves of the pandemic.

In terms of the sample of cases under attention, this book's empirical analyses will refer to liberal democratic countries according to whether they are in the Global North or South. This distinction, importantly, is not based on whether a given country is located below the line of the equator – the "South" has typically denoted whether a country is broadly in the regions of Latin America, Asia, Africa, and Oceania (Dados & Connell, p. 12). This distinction arose through "an allegorical application of categories to name patterns of wealth, privilege, and development across broad regions" and the term "South" tends to function as a metaphor for underdevelopment along with histories of colonialism, imperialism, and what Dados & Connell refer to as differential economic and social change (Dados & Connell, p. 13). The Global North/South distinction also stems to geopolitical relations of power and numerous ideas that have been theorized to account for why there are either "developed" or "underdeveloped" countries; why there are "first," "second," or "third" world countries; why there are "core" or "periphery" countries. After the end of the Cold War, academic discourse shifted into categorizing states as belonging to either the "Global North" or the "Global South" and these concepts gained "increased sophistication" throughout intellectual movements and offered new trajectories across the world (Dados & Connell, p. 12).

Below, Figure 3.1 illustrates the size of populations across all countries. Data are drawn from the World Bank based on the year 2022. This figure, along with the following figure (3.2) were visualized in the R Programming language (R 4.3.0).

This book draws from many different sources of data to try to paint a comprehensive picture of characteristics that are associated with each of the countries under attention. For qualitative comparative or simply qualitative parts of my empirical analyses, I accessed and relied on translated information (through the translational application, DeepL) or through governmental institutions' reports that were provided in the English language. Considering that the pandemic took place very recently and was markedly impactful on international travel, to the benefit of this book's research design, every single country that is in the sample of cases provided English based versions of its rules and regulations that were enforced throughout different waves of the pandemic. In this respect, qualitative research on the pandemic was very straightforward and easier than usual for contexts wherein English is not the native or state language.

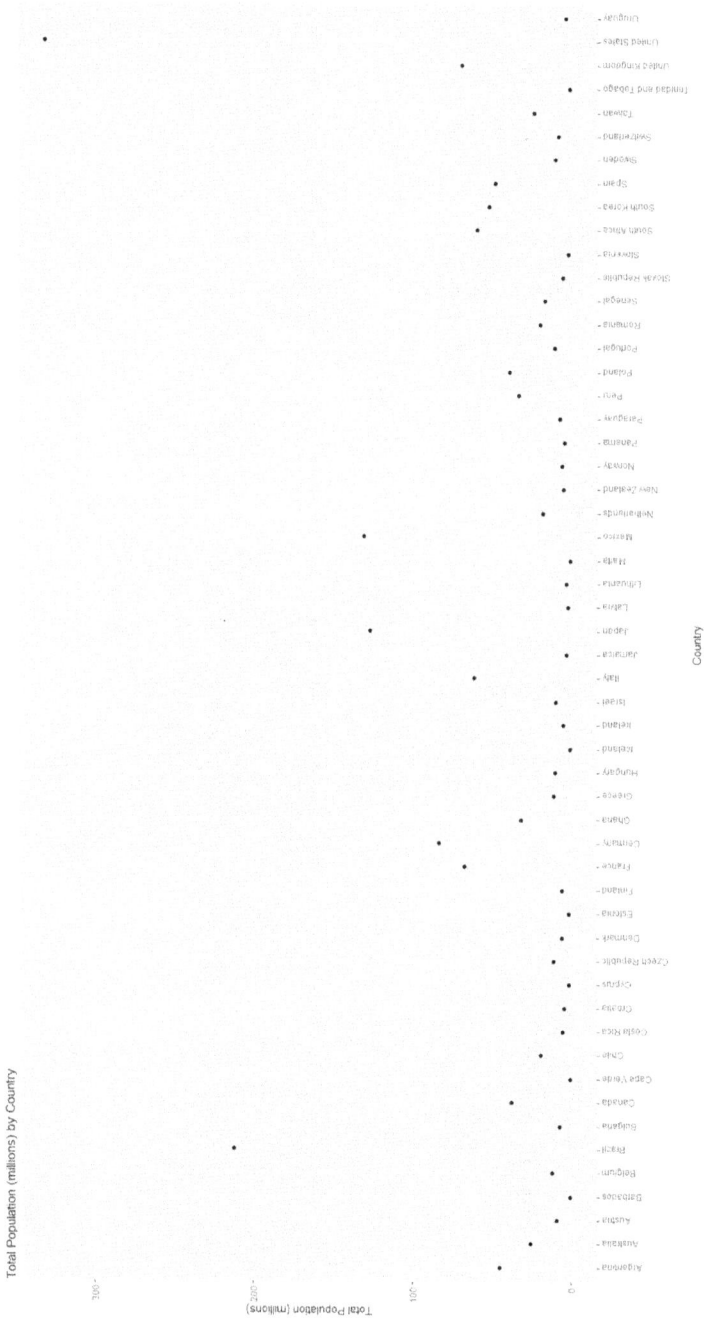

Figure 3.1: Total Population by Country (n=54)

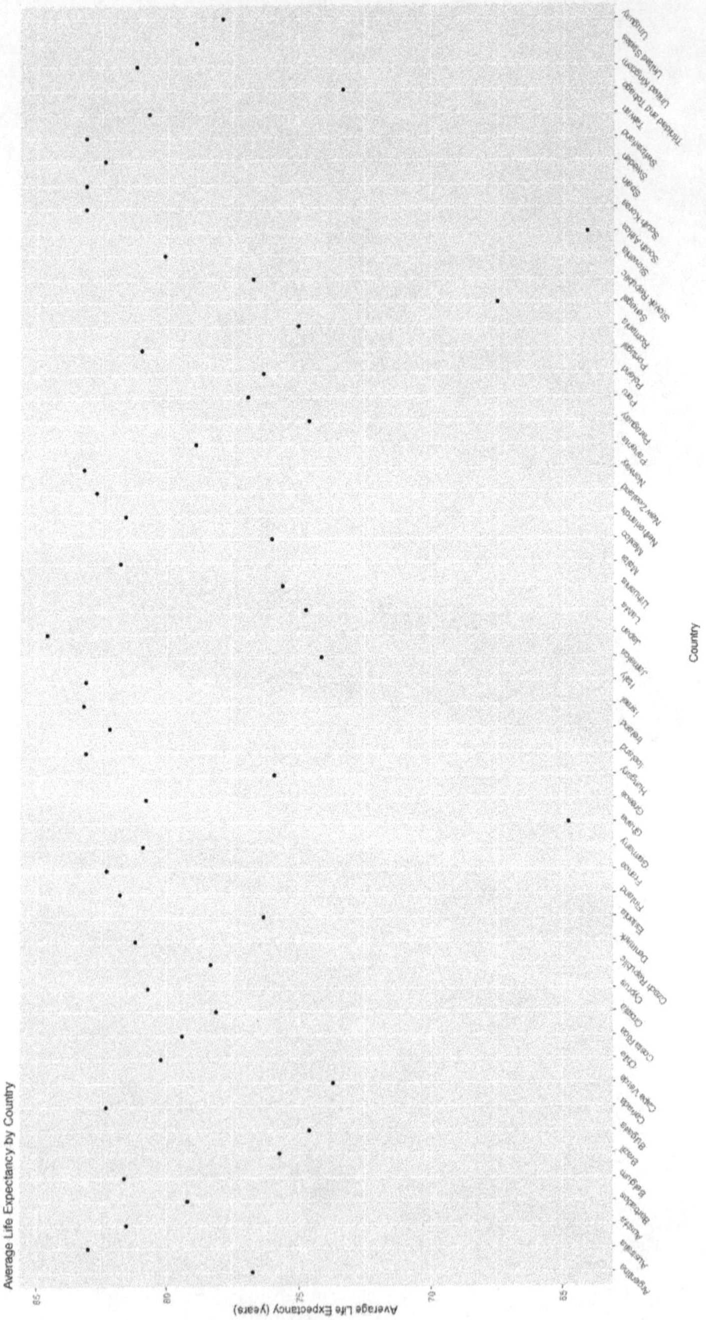

Figure 3.2: Average Life Expectancy (n=54)

Chapter 4: Waves of the Pandemic

A woman enters a tramcar wearing a thick wool jacket, winter hat, and an N95 facemask. She sits down right as the tramcar makes an abrupt stop. A fender-bender accident involving two cars occurred just up the street and traffic is now at a standstill. The operator of the tramcar makes an announcement which details an expected delay. The woman pulls out her smartphone and notices that everyone else in proximity are glaring down at their smartphones. Shortly after, another announcement is made by the operator and this time, the doors of the tramcar open and passengers are given the opportunity to leave. A cold wind blows into the tramcar and all passengers remain seated, drawn to their smartphones. 15 minutes pass as the woman finally steps out of the tramcar and begins to walk the final stretch of her journey to work. Glancing back, the woman sees reflections of brightly lit electronic devices on the window of the tramcar. She then heads to her favorite pre-work destination, a coffee and pastry shop. Here, she presents her COVID-19 vaccination QR code which is scanned form her smartphone by an employee who was standing at the door, making sure only valid QR-code holding individuals can enter the coffee shop. Little did the woman know that most of her life was being tracked on her handheld supercomputer. Her internet browsing history, geolocation movement history, call history, social media contacts, and health parameters from her smartwatch (that was synched to an app in her smartphone), all contained information that was not private to her individual self. This information is a valuable commodity – a commodity that is consistently syphoned into data collection systems by third party applications.

At the height of the COVID-19 pandemic, informational databases were composed, monitored, and analyzed by governments and particular state institutions such as ministries of health, security services, and police. This chapter will delve into a temporal historical analysis of the five waves that made up the COVID-19 pandemic. I begin with the first wave and end with the fifth and carry out an in-depth inquiry into a heterogeneous set of restrictions and regulations through specific observation of the country context of the Czech Republic and also reference other states that fall into the sample under attention in this book. The Czech Republic, analogous to dozens of other EU countries, saw its incumbent government and policy makers carry out policies that were similar to nearby states. The first vaccines that were made in response to COVID-19 emerged around April of 2021 and were administered to at risk groups which included elderly segments of populations and those with known or established co-morbidities to influenza-like viruses. As the weeks and months went on, most Western states experienced a rapid trajectory in which vaccines were unveiled, sent out, and administered to

https://doi.org/10.1515/9783111345703-004

populations. Vaccination of at-risk age groups was first carried out and then trickled down to young adults who were offered the opportunity to get a first dose of vaccination.

At the tail end of the first wave of the pandemic, alongside the rolling out of vaccines for COVID-19, the EU created a system called "getaway" which tracked cross-border movement and in turn, enabled governments of member states to quarantine and trace geolocation patterns of civilians based on large-scale digital tech infrastructure and data structures (Anisin, 2022c, p. 46). Here, all but one of the 27 EU member states (France), created and implemented mobile/smartphone-based tracking systems (Anisin, 2022c, p. 47). These systems were created in time of state of emergency or during emergency decrees that were passed on national levels throughout member states and then policies on enforcing the tracking of civilians fizzled downwards to regional, municipal, and local governing and security institutions. Although the technological response to the pandemic was unprecedented, it was not the first attempt that human beings have taken to regulate infectious disease. Infectious diseases have always had a tendency to cast individuals into being societal outliers.

Pandemics and Infectious Disease, A Brief History

For a collection of different reasons human societies have always seemed to discriminate against individuals and groups suffering from severe infectious disease. Between 1000 and 1250 throughout Europe, leprosy became the subject of both ecclesiastical and legal intervention (Hays, 2009, p. 23). This resulted in those who suffered from leprosy to be objected to laws that severed them away from society. Sufferers experienced ostracization and were legally sanctioned (Hays, 2009, p. 23). Even though authorities (and society more broadly) had no idea about the root cause of leprosy (i.e., debates surrounded whether leprosy was contagious, hereditary, or was contracted due to a person's sinful behavior), lepers were forced to wear a black veil over their faces and had to frequently encounter priests who would read them prohibitive statements out loud. Lepers were forbidden from: leaving their own home without their leper costume/attire; from touching anything they wanted to buy; from entering a tavern; from giving anything to children; from drinking or eating from dishes other than their own; from eating or drinking in company, unless with other lepers (Hays, 2009, p. 24). As readers may acknowledge, these characteristics sound awfully familiar.

Into the Middle Ages, the notion that leprosy was contagious became more prominent amongst the Church, which resulted in what Hays (2009) refers to as a doctrine of contagion. By the 14th century, the bubonic plague wiped out a large percentage of the European population and became known as the Black Death. Throughout the variant stages of the plague and its aftermath, victims and their families would be forced to confine to their homes (for example, in Florence), with doors locked and were barred from going outside (Hays, 2009, p. 55). Plague "pesthouses" as Hays (2009) describes them, were set up in towns which led to substantial civic expenses. Attempts at regulating disease in the Middle Ages and then throughout the onset of industrialization were, nevertheless, bound to fail. Scientists had not yet discovered bacteria, there were very few medicinal options available for viruses and bacterial illnesses, and vaccinations did not exist. Indeed, COVID-19 is far less lethal than the bubonic plague – estimates place the latter to have wiped out 50 – 60 % of the entire European population (Benedictow, 2005), while the former appeared to have claimed less than 1 % per annum. In 2020, Italy was among the first nations to be hit hard by COVID-19 – tens of millions of Italians were forced to lockdown and were not allowed to leave their apartments and homes for substantial durations of time. As Italy was the first European country hit by the pandemic (Romano et al., 2022), mass media coverage of the Italian lockdown was so profound that one could not avoid hearing about or encountering public discussions about how Italians were failing to cope with overfilled intensive care units.

By the time the first and second waves of the pandemic were ongoing, many countries in the sample of cases under attention in this book, such as Australia, developed a quarantine hotel system because government facilities did not have enough capacity to quarantine travelers who were coming from abroad. Australia introduced a 14-day quarantine for travelers who had arrived from another country – most quarantines were carried out in private hotels through isolation policies. The latter are described by Dincer & Gocer (2021) as being constitutive of a "quarantine journey" which was regulated by each regional body in Australia. The journey began with guests arriving and being allocated buses, transferred to different hotels (by police escorts), and then placed in specified hotel rooms for 14 days. Guests were informed by a lengthy government brochure that, "quarantining in a hotel will be different from your normal experience of staying in a hotel", and could be challenging" (Dincer & Gocer, 2021, p. 3).

Shifting back over to the EU context, in Romano et al.'s (2022) inquiry into Italian and Spanish media, the authors explore daily newspaper front pages and argue that front page news headlines were graphic and turned out to be effective in terms of their ability to serve as a privileged space for the construction of public identity. Over the course of February 24 to April 4, 2020, COVID-19 related information occupied 71 % of all front-page news headlines (62 % in Spain and 80 % in Italy) – with the most common type of headline being categorized as a brief, followed by news, then opinion pieces. The authors find that of the types of headlines that were most common, "appellative" content was by far the most significant – surpassing both "informative" and "expressive" content. Appellative content is described by the authors as being focused on drawing reader attention and that such "the headlines tend to be non-verbal and have very atomized structures that seek to convey to the reader news about a subject he or she already knows" (Romano et al., 2022, p. 6).

Just as during the plague when "trade would stop, workers might be confined to their homes, stocks of material might be seized and burnt" (Hays, 2009, p. 55), upwards of 100 different countries around the global, including Italy, experienced extreme restrictions on social interactions and economic activity in 2020 some of which then stemmed into 2021 and even into the early portion of 2022. The following types of restrictions and regulations were incorporated in attempt to slow down the spread of COVID-19: school closures; workplace closures; cancellation of public events; restrictions on public gatherings; closures of public transport; stay-at-home requirements; restrictions on movement; and international travel control (Hale et al., 2021). The following table features data drawn from the Oxford Coronavirus Government Response Tracker (OxCGRT) project and the noted stringency index for each country under attention.

Table 4.1: Stringency Index (n=54)

Country	Stringency Index
Austria	73.89
Belgium	78.21
Brazil	52.11
Bulgaria	65.28
Canada	68.92
Croatia	62.56
Cyprus	72.3
Czech Republic	75.01
Denmark	77.84
Estonia	70.15
Finland	72.03
France	77.75
Germany	75.89
Greece	70.95
Hungary	68.71
Iceland	68.78
Ireland	75.41
Israel	73.22
Italy	73.93
Jamaica	61.49

Table 4.1: Stringency Index (n=54) *(Continued)*

Country	Stringency Index
Japan	69.07
Latvia	71.01
Lithuania	71.67
Malta	74.02
Mexico	57.84
Netherlands	76.22
Norway	73.45
Poland	64.99
Portugal	72.12
Romania	62.47
Slovak Republic	68.48
Slovenia	71.78
South Korea	70.53
Spain	74.16
Sweden	68.15
Switzerland	75.21
United Kingdom	76.85
United States	66.43
Argentina	62.32
Australia	70.72
Barbados	62.08
Chile	67.22
Cape Verde	54.65
Costa Rica	63.84
Ghana	50.92
New Zealand	71.63
Panama	62.17
Peru	57.32
Senegal	53.29
South Africa	58.39
Taiwan	68.73
Trinidad and Tobago	61.97
Uruguay	67.67
Paraguay	58.76

Wave One, January-April 2020

A hegemonic narrative surrounding the outbreak of the COVID-19 pandemic tells us that the outbreak of the virus occurred sometime in December 2019 in Wuhan China. Reports by high profile news outlets began to circulate about a new and severe form of respiratory illness that was highly contagious and spreading throughout a highly populated area of China. By January 30, 2020, the World Health Organization formally declared that COVID-19 constituted a major public health emergency that was of international concern. In this early period of the first wave, the WHO began to prescribe policy guidelines for countries in order to stop or slow down the transmission of the virus: as noted by the director, "If countries detect, test, treat, isolate, trace, and mobilize their people in the response, those with a handful of cases can prevent those cases becoming clusters, and those clusters becoming community transmission" (World Health Organization, 2020a).

Although China went into full lockdown by mid-January of 2020, a significant number of international flights had already been departing (and arriving) from the country's major international transport hubs. By this point, it was already too late to actually prevent the global spread of COVID-19. Early variants of the virus were very infectious and more importantly, the virus was highly efficient in terms of reproducing itself and spreading from host to host which is in stark contrast to more lethal types of viruses and diseases such as Ebola (which kills its host very quickly, and hence, has a lesser likelihood of spreading into a pandemic). By the end of February, the WHO put out a "Situation Report" (no. 40), which highlighted the rampant spread of the virus to 53 countries and its risk assessment was classified as "Very High" (World Health Organization, 2020b). This report also featured a link to *Rational use of personal protective equipment for coronavirus disease 2019 (COVID-19)*, which ended up being disseminated to governments throughout the world with subsequent updates. This document's "interim guidance" featured a description of the "most effective preventive measures in the community" which include (World Health Organization, 2020c):

- performing hand hygiene frequently with an alcohol-based hand rub if your hands are not visibly dirty or with soap and water if hands are dirty;
- avoiding touching your eyes, nose and mouth;
- practicing respiratory hygiene by coughing or sneezing into a bent elbow or tissue and then immediately disposing of the tissue;
- wearing a medical mask if you have respiratory symptoms and performing hand hygiene after disposing of the mask;
- maintaining social distance (a minimum of 1 m) from individuals with respiratory symptoms.

The brief then detailed the types of interactions that should be permitted in different areas of society, including hospitals (and different parts of hospitals), in communities, schools, trains, malls, homes, and the broad category of "anywhere." Simultaneously, countries that had already detected cases of the virus began to create policies based on the WHO's recommendations. In February 2020 one of the commissioners of the European Council, Stella Kyriakides, stressed the need for cooperation among EU member states with Brussels in order to "produce a model for information for travelers coming back from risk areas or traveling to them – information we see an increased need for within the EU" (Anisin, 2022c, p. 47). This led to the rapid formation of a European health tracking system that functioned through surveillance capitalistic logics. By April of 2020, the EU Commission's report titled, "Guidance on Apps Supporting the Fight against COVID-19 Pandemic in Relation to Data Protection" described how digital technologies "have a valuable role to play in combatting the COVID-19 crisis" and how these applications can support public health authorities on both national (member state) and supranational (European wide) levels to engage in contract tracing (Anisin, 2022c, p. 49). A key dynamic here pertains to contact tracing – during the first wave of the pandemic, the idea of contact tracing not only arose, but gained widespread prominence and acceptance by policy makers and politicians. Contract tracing was rolled out through sophisticated technological instruments that relied on individuals' smartphones and their geolocation histories. This is where things became illiberal and murky.

Geolocation functions are voluntary on each individual smartphone if observed according to Android and IOS instructions – an individual can turn off his/her geolocation on their smartphone at any moment they desire, and all applications that rely on geolocation ask users for their permission to use their geolocation data. Yet time has shown that these technologies in smartphones can be accessed by third parties without user permission. Over the course of the last decade, a number of high-profile news articles were published that detailed how the NSA (United States National Security Agency) had been tracking millions of smartphones through their geolocation functions and through mobile phone network towers. The NYT's editorial board put forward a "Privacy Project" in late 2019 in a report titled, "Total Surveillance Is Not What America Signed Up For" (The New York Times, 2019). The report detailed a long stemming investigation and the compilation of dataset on smartphone-based surveillance which was provided to journalists "by sources alarmed by the power of the tracking industry." Upwards of 50 billion location datapoints were collected on millions of Americans across major urban areas – the report reveals that through these datapoints, it is possible to track specific movements of both high-profile actors and regular people, ranging from President Trump's secret service guards to protesters. Arguably the most significant aspect of the report (which is tough to not agree with) can be summarized in the following quote,

In most cases, it was child's play for them to connect a supposedly anonymous data trail to a name and an address – to a real live human being. Your smartphone can broadcast your exact location thousands of times per day, through hundreds of apps, instantaneously to dozens of different companies. Each of those companies has the power to follow individual mobile phones wherever they go, in near-real time. That's not a glitch in the system. It is the system. If the government ordered Americans to continuously provide such precise, real-time information about themselves, there would be a revolt. Members of Congress would trample one another to be first in front of the cable news cameras to quote the founders and insist on our rights to be free of such pervasive surveillance. Yet, as a society, without ever focusing on this profound choice, we've reached a tacit consensus to hand this data over voluntarily, even though we don't really know who's getting it or what they're doing with it (The New York Times, 2019).

These practices are also not solely an American phenomenon but are likely contingent on state capacity – meaning that states with significant strength in their security institutions have enough resources to engage in mass surveillance over their populaces. For instance, Iran has an entire security agency known as the Basij which is comprised of dozens of different branches, some of which are entirely detected to surveillance of political opposition. China has even more extensive surveillance capacities. As a slight contrast, in liberal democratic contexts, states also obviously have surveillance capacities – the caveat here is that populaces who are governed by democratically elected leaders are either fully unaware that their behaviors and personal lives are being tracked for the purposes of upholding political status quos, state security, or for the benign purpose of consumerist-profit seeking across the vast realm of digital commerce. During the first two waves of the pandemic, very sophisticated surveillance systems were set up via state security institutions who either gained control over or were principally in charge of informational flows of applications that relied on private technological corporation and companies' data infrastructure.

April marked the end of the first wave of the pandemic. By the end of this month, the WHO had already issued its 101st Situation Report which detailed the global spread of the virus – the highest totals of confirmed cases were listed according to region. This was also the point at which surveillance applications were created for the purpose of digital contact tracing. One of the earliest scholarly articles on the ethics of digital contact tracing was published in the prestigious journal, *Science* (Ferretti et al., 2020), in May of 2020. This article presented several analytical approaches to attempt to quantify COVID-19 infection and transmission rates. The article also offered one of the first and most widely read ethical considerations of what digital contract tracing should entail, with the first characteristic being that "appropriate use" of an app must rely on commanding and "well-founded public trust and confidence." Ferretti et al., (2020) also stressed the importance of establishing oversight of application functions by "an inclusive and transparent advisory board which includes members of the public." What's more, the authors argued that, "people should be democratically entitled to decide whether to adopt this platform." The obvious issues with these recommendations are that publics in liberal democracies ended up being completely removed from digital contract tracing and surveillance policies. They were: 1) not asked about whether they would like to participate in digital contact tracing; 2) were not consulted on what digital contact tracing entails for their personal privacy; 3) were not invited to participate in any advisory board that would oversee how such applications would function in real time or retrospectively.

What did end up happening was that digital contact tracing was used by liberal democratic governments and state security institutions to not only identify individuals that had tested positive for COVID-19, but to track and surveillance other individuals who could have come in contact with them according to a given set of proximity parameters.

In Israel, contact tracing applications were used (already in 2020) to spy on and track civilians through its main state security institution, the Mossad along with other affiliated organs such as the Shin Bet (Holmes, 2020). By December 2020, it became known that these applications had been used to target political opponents, such as ethnic Arabs in Jerusalem where civil rights lawyers had received messages such as the following, "You have been spotted as having participated in acts of violence in the Al-Aqsa Mosque," it read in Arabic. "We will hold you accountable" (Burke et al., 2022). Hundreds of other civil rights lawyers received similar messages, but not because of their involvement in any radical organization. These individuals had lived or worked in a neighborhood in which there was political unrest – for these reasons, the Shin Bet flagged them through the pandemic-based surveillance technology and directly targeted them with coercion. As noted by a detailed report put out by the Associated Press, "from Beijing to Jerusalem to Hyderabad, India, and Perth, Australia, The Associated Press has found that authorities used these technologies and data to halt travel for activists and ordinary people, harass marginalized communities and link people's health information to other surveillance and law enforcement tools. In some cases, data was shared with spy agencies" (Burke et al., 2022).

In Hong Kong, the usage of surveillance applications that were created for the purpose of monitoring infection rates during the pandemic were later used to repress political opposition. Specifically, covid-based surveillance applications fostered what activists and journalists described as a "golden opportunity" to track and trace potential pro-democracy protesters (Davidson, 2020). The government forced individuals to wear digital wristbands which enabled it to obtain a large number of data reference points on individuals' geo-locations and movements.

These data were not limited to individuals who were forced to quarantine, as the arrest of high-profile activists arose at the points in which these systems were rolled out. In the US context, during the beginning segments of the pandemic (in 2020), individuals in some US states (such as Kentucky) who broke quarantine rules were ordered to wear GPS-based tracking devices. Louisville's city chief of public services, Amy Hess, stated that while she would prefer that usage of such devices would not be needed, state law in Kentucky enabled home confinement to be "imposed" for the purpose of protecting public health (Satter, 2020). Analogous policies were being discussed in Hawaii and in West Virginia.

Similar albeit more wide-reaching surveillance processes arose around the same time in India which comparatively had the largest total number of people under lockdown and were monitored by an application called Aarogya Setu (translated to Health Bridge) – the application was mandatory for all employees in public and private sectors to download and use (Phartiyal, 2020). A fascinating dynamic here pertains to the requirement that India's Ministry of Home Affairs placed upon individuals at the outset of the launch of this application – this institution publicly declared "to ensure 100 % coverage of this app among the employees" (Phartiyal, 2020). As of May 2020, the application was downloaded upwards of 50 million times via the Google Play Store.

To enforce the usage of these applications, governments enacted emergency decrees and as the subsequent chapter of this book will reveal, they repeatedly extended state of emergencies for months, and in some contexts, for years on end. Throughout 2020 and most of 2021, liberal democratic states also relied on drone technology to engage in physical crowd control and track if individuals and communities were abiding by lockdown measures. In Spain, "aerial surveillance" had already been carried out in early March of 2020 to enforce the government's state of emergency. For those who broke or breached the regulations of the shutdown, individuals faced fines of up to 600,000 Euros and up to a year in prison (Doffman, 2020). In England, drones were also operated (Recine, 2020).

These examples are obviously not comprehensive of the immense breadth of surveillance that was carried out throughout the height of the pandemic across liberal democratic states and societies. In April of 2020 both Apple and Google announced that they were working on Bluetooth technology interoperability between Android and iOS devices "to empower coronavirus tracking apps for smartphones" (Johnson, 2020). The specific joint statement they put out stressed the importance of user privacy, yet did not specify how it could be feasibly achieved. Part of the statement noted that,

> in the coming months, Apple and Google will work to enable a broader Bluetooth-based contact tracing platform by building this functionality into the underlying platforms. This is a

more robust solution than an API and would allow more individuals to participate, if they choose to opt in, as well as enable interaction with a broader ecosystem of apps and government health authorities. Privacy, transparency, and consent are of utmost importance in this effort, and we look forward to building this functionality in consultation with interested stakeholders. We will openly publish information about our work for others to analyze (Apple, 2020).

The empirical manifestation of these applications, unfortunately, was not able to prevent the spread of the virus nor slow down rates of infection. Instead, the virus continued to mutate and new strains emerged and meanwhile, entire populations were placed on lockdowns while their movement (via geolocation data) was being extensively monitored by state security institutions and law enforcement. This was precisely accomplished through the broad framework of "contact tracing" which was built on complex Bluetooth technologies that are described in a technical manual that was put forward alongside the formal public statements made by both of these tech conglomerates. This manual titled, "Exposure Notification" was put out as an appendix link in the aforementioned statement by Google and Apple. The April 2020 v1.2 report laid out the technical specifications of contact tracing and noted,

> Exposure Notification makes it possible to combat the spread of the coronavirus – the pathogen that causes COVID-19 – by alerting participants about possible exposure to someone they have recently been in contact with, who has subsequently been positively diagnosed as having the virus. The Exposure Notification Service is the vehicle for implementing exposure notification and uses the Bluetooth Low Energy wireless technology for proximity detection of nearby smartphones, and for the data exchange mechanism (Google, 2020).

Tools were created for the purpose of Bluetooth-based contact tracing and are described in the report as being safeguarded to protect individual privacy. The issue here is that data that were gathered through the architecture of these applications could then be used for whatever reason deemed necessary by governments. Centralized applications that were used for contact tracing in places such as Singapore and Australia enabled data to be drawn from user's phones and then sent to central databases which were controlled by national health institutions (Sharon, 2020).

As Sharon (2020) argues, the digital currency that both Apple and Google possess has made headway into new spheres and poses specific risks that are not captured in their privacy policies. What's more, these companies' applications have obtained such wide-reaching usage throughout the world that they also have encroached into the sphere of politics which runs risk of fostering new dependencies on corporate actors for public goods to be delivered (Sharon, 2020, p. 46). Along similar lines, Hoepman (2020) argues that the API Google/Apple put out in April 2020 easily could be expanded to centralized forms of contact tracing. This plat-

form can be triangulated with other applications rather easily and can inform potentially malicious actors or parties on swaths of individuals' movement and behavioral patterns.

The table below features information on all COVID-19 contact tracing apps that
were created either in the first or second waves of the pandemic. As evident, all
countries in the sample had such applications created.

Table 4.2: COVID-19 Contact Tracing Applications (n=54)

Country	COVID-19 Contact Tracing App	Date of Implementation
Austria	Stopp Corona	03/25/20
Belgium	Coronalert	09/30/20
Brazil	Coronavirus-SUS	08/05/20
Bulgaria	ViruSafe	06/15/20
Canada	COVID Alert	07/31/20
Croatia	Stop COVID-19	07/10/20
Cyprus	COVTRACING	06/15/20
Czech Republic	eRouška	03/18/20
Denmark	Smittestop	06/18/20
Estonia	HOIA	08/20/20
Finland	Koronavilkku	09/01/20
France	TousAntiCovid	10/22/20
Germany	Corona-Warn-App	06/16/20
Greece	COVID Radar	07/28/20
Hungary	VírusRadar	04/22/20
Iceland	Rakning C-19	04/01/20
Ireland	COVID Tracker	07/07/20
Israel	HaMagen	03/22/20
Italy	Immuni	06/01/20
Jamaica	JamCOVID	03/01/20
Japan	COCOA	06/19/20
Latvia	Apturi COVID	04/02/20
Lithuania	COVID-19 LT	04/07/20
Malta	COVID Alert Malta	07/07/20
Mexico	COVID-19 MX	06/11/20
Netherlands	CoronaMelder	09/01/20
Norway	Smittestopp	06/15/20
Poland	ProteGO Safe	06/18/20
Portugal	STAYAWAY COVID	09/01/20
Romania	COVID-19 RO	06/15/20
Slovak Republic	eKaranténa	03/23/20
Slovenia	#OstaniZdrav	06/18/20
South Korea	Self-quarantine Safety App	05/01/20
Spain	Radar COVID	08/10/20
Sweden	Smittestopp	06/15/20

Table 4.2: COVID-19 Contact Tracing Applications (n=54) *(Continued)*

Country	COVID-19 Contact Tracing App	Date of Implementation
Switzerland	SwissCovid	06/25/20
United Kingdom	NHS COVID-19	09/24/20
United States	Various	Varies by state
Argentina	Cuidar	04/01/20
Australia	COVIDSafe	04/26/20
Barbados	BIMSafe	07/21/20
Chile	COVID-19 Chile	06/15/20
Cape Verde	VACINE CV	01/01/21
Costa Rica	Pura Vida	11/01/20
Ghana	GH COVID-19 Tracker App	04/13/20
New Zealand	NZ COVID Tracer	05/20/20
Panama	Radar COVID Panamá	11/01/20
Peru	Perú en tus manos	05/01/20
Senegal	Suivi COVID Senegal	06/02/20
South Africa	COVID Alert SA	09/01/20
Taiwan	Taiwan Social Distancing App	04/01/20
Trinidad and Tobago	Trinidad and Tobago COVID-19 App	05/01/20
Uruguay	Coronavirus UY	04/01/20
Paraguay	AsisT	06/01/20

An interesting observation can be made simply from some of the names that these applications were given, specifically those that featured the word "stop." This is emblematic of the Chinese approach to the pandemic with its "zero-COVID" policy. This highly authoritative approach to dealing with public health is disconcerting. Even with the most successful medicinal interventions into infectious viruses such as the historical creation of vaccination for measles (in 1963), there still are over one hundred thousand people who die from the virus each year on average (at the time of writing this book), and what's more, over the course of the last half century, at its height, measles caused an estimated 2.6 million deaths each year (World Health Organization, 2023a). The notion that a respiratory virus can be "stopped" is problematic to say the least.

The Second Wave, April 2020-November 2020

The beginning of the second wave of the pandemic was marked by discussions that were circulating throughout public discourse on when and if vaccines would become available; on restrictions; on home schooling; working from home, among other issues that pertained to what at that point in time were the most substantial shutdowns of societal activity in human history. To exemplify the extent of restrictions that were enforced at the beginning of the second wave of the pandemic across much of the Global North, the context of the Czech Republic and its extended state of emergency will be drawn on. At the time of enforcement, restrictions were often described as "extraordinary measures," and indeed they were extraordinary when they were first implemented because such wide reaching interferences into personal and public life had never been carried out on as large of a scale, but as subsequent sections of this chapter will reveal, as time went on, restrictions were reinforced and rearticulated at such a frequency that the extraordinary nature of the emergency decrees became standard. In late March of 2020, the Czech Republic approved a range of "anti-crisis measures" along with a new debt ceiling for the state budget deficit, the following enforcements prolonged regulations on retail and service sales; prohibition of public presence in restaurants; the closure of office spaces; closure of schools; a 14-day quarantine for those who have come abroad (Government of the Czech Republic, 2020a)

On March 30, 2020, a "smart quarantine" project was launched and retrospectively, around three years later, it is clear that this was the precise moment in time that governments rolled out not only policies that were authoritarian liberal in nature, but applications that were created through surveillance capitalistic technologies and resources. The state had set up a "COVID-19 Central Management Team" that would lead a "smart quarantine" project. It had also extended the ban on foreigners (without a residence permit) from entering the country (Government of the Czech Republic, 2020b). Moreover, the ban on free movement throughout the country was extended as was the ban on retail sales and services, restaurants and catering facilities, and above all, no more than two individuals could be together in any given public place at any given moment in time. Apart from children younger than the age of two, all individuals who went out in public had to wear facemasks. The government report that first revealed the smart quarantine project justified its creation through the following statements,

> The Government wants to use this modern information-technology project to search faster and more efficiently for people who could be infected with COVID-19. As of today, the project is being tested in the South Moravian Region. The Army of the Czech Republic is helping significantly with its implementation. With effect from 30 March the Government has approved the deployment of 300 soldiers into active service. They will be assisting with sample collection and other work on this project (Government of the Czech Republic, 2020b).

The next emergency Press Advisory report was put out on April 6, 2020 and here, the state allowed individuals to exercise alone outside without facemasks and opened up "essential travel" for individuals needing to leave the country. More than two individuals could not gather outside at any given point in time and people who go shopping must keep two or more meters away from another (Government of the Czech Republic, 2020c). Just three days later after this press release, the government extended the state of emergency until April 30. By April 24 individuals could go outside in groups up to 10 people. Then on April 27, church services were allowed to be held "under strict hygienic conditions" but only with a maximum of 15 persons. Interestingly enough, at this point in time, there were no restrictions on the total number of people that could enter large supermarkets for shopping. This is a key authoritarian liberal dynamic that will be addressed in the sixth chapter of this book.

Into May of 2020, many restrictions began to ease, most of which surrounded social distancing and mask wearing, and as the summer season moved closer, greater numbers of people were allowed to participate in outdoor areas and attractions such as zoos or botanical gardens. During this time, state security institutions closely monitored rates of infection across different parts of the country through a "traffic light system" that was used to divide different districts by color based on infection rates. By September, most of the Northern hemisphere began to experience the annual uptick in colds and viruses that tend to arise with the change of seasons and, once again, a state of emergency was initiated and many public events were closed as were catering and food facilities. In early October 2020, a shift back to group-limitations both indoors (10 people maximum) and outdoors (20 people maximum) was made and as the month went on, restrictions began to intensify. On October 22, "the free movement of persons throughout the Czech Republic" became prohibited. The only possible way that someone could leave their area or zone in which their residence (primary home) is located was to take trips for work or business, to see family, purchase "basic necessities" or take trips for healthcare facilities.

This leads us to measures that to the best of my knowledge, were the most extreme measures in the history of population control in a liberal democratic polity. The aforementioned status of a state of emergency continuously was extended (each month) into 2021 and by the latter half of 2020, polities across the EU took measures to fully restrict movement according to parameters that hitherto were difficult to imagine.

The Third Wave, November 2020-May 2021

Sticking with the Czech context, on November 2, 2020 free movement of persons was prohibited from 9 p.m. to 4:59 a.m. apart from the following exceptions: 1. travel to work and for the purpose of carrying out business or other similar activities and for carrying out the duties of a public official or constitutional authority and back to their place of residence; 2. performing their occupation; 3. performing activities serving to ensure a) security, internal order and the resolution of the crisis situation, b) protection of health, provision of medical or social care; c) public transit and other infrastructure, d) services for citizens including supply and delivery services, 4. urgent trips that are necessary even at night due to the protection of life, health, assets or other statutorily protected interests; 5. walking dogs within 500 meters of their place of residence (Government of the Czech Republic, 2020d).

The second set of restrictions that were enforced on November 2 only permitted the following categories of free movement of persons from 5:00 a.m. to 20:59 p.m.: 1) travel to work and for the purpose of carrying out business or other similar activities and for carrying out the duties of a public official or constitutional authority, 2. essential travel to visit family or close persons, 3. essential travel to procure basic essentials (shopping for groceries, medicine and medical devices, hygienic products, cosmetics or other drug store goods, animal food and other animal supplies), including essentials for relatives and close persons, assuring child care, assuring animal care, using the necessary financial and postal services, refueling, waste disposal, travel required for ensuring the needs and services for another. During this time period, the EU recommended member states ban travel from non-EU countries and this ban was then widely implemented based on an "international traffic light system" that categorized states according to their reported rates of infection.

Into December of 2020, states of emergencies across many liberal democratic countries were still in place after having been repeatedly extended over the course of nearly the entire year. On December 3, all shops and services were allowed to open under specific conditions of social distancing and the presentation of a negative antigen or PCR test (depending on the type of shop or location). The same day saw the Czech government lift a ban on alcohol consumption in public and a previous ban on Sunday shopping. Several restrictions pertaining to free movement were removed only to then be reimposed on December 18. A week before Christmas, bars, restaurants, zoos, museums, swimming pools and all indoor facilities were closed once again (Government of the Czech Republic, 2020c). At the turn of 2021, all emergency measures were extended – until January 22. Restrictions on free movement, on services, on public administration services, on public gatherings, and leaving one's residence were once again executed. On January 19, 2021, the government announced an extension to the state of emergency until February 14. A new state of emergency then was implemented until March 28. During this time, the government declared that individuals who sought to go outside could only do so in a surgical mask or an N95 respirator. Into March 2021, these mask wearing rules only intensified as N95 respirators became the only acceptable type of face covering that could be worn in public.

This brings us to the height of the second wave of the pandemic – March 2021. At this point in time, it became forbidden for individuals to leave either the district they lived in or the city – without what the Ministry of Health declared to be "good reason such as travel to work or to a doctor" (Government of the Czech Republic, 2020c). The determining of "good reason" here is critical, as states (i.e., not only the Czech Republic) articulated what a "good" justification for leaving one's home would entail. Across Europe, these decisions symbolized societies' entrenchment into capitalistic economic structures. Human beings were reduced to workers because the only activity they could pursue in the real world (outside of their homes) literally and physically entailed formal types of employment. Individuals could only leave their homes for work (or for medical care). This complements the authoritarian liberal economic logic of optimizing economic outcomes during a crisis.

In light of the numerous crises sparked by COVID-19, governments sought to optimize economic outcomes over all other outcomes which included socio-cultural activities, personal relationships, spirituality (e.g., religious practices), sports, and all forms of recreation that require being outdoors or in facilities that are not a part of one's home. Interestingly enough, for the small percentages of individuals who own extensive land, property, and have recreational facilities within their own homes, these restrictions were not as detrimental as they were for the majority of people. The former could enjoy recreation within their own property and home, while the latter were forced to make ends meet in the confines of small living spaces, often crammed and not suitable for at-home schooling, work, and other activities. An interesting characteristic of these harsh regulations can be observed in a stipulation that was enforced on March 1, 2021 which stated that if people own a holiday home, they can visit it, but once they arrive, then the place will be considered their place of residence – meaning that they could then not leave the holiday home.

Most importantly, one cannot assign any plausible degree of medical rationality to the hegemonic policy of restricting all activities except formal work. That individuals could only leave their homes to go work exemplifies the authoritarian liberal basis of contemporary socio-political order in democracies. Such a restriction clearly benefited economic aspects of society at the detriment of all others. It reveals the intrinsic structural basis of current societies – to keep consistent positive economic growth, economic activity, and to protect individuals' ability of selling one's labor or time for the greater aim of profit. As Kropotkin (2015) noted more than a century ago, such a society is highly antagonistic to cooperation for human beings, and is also markedly different than any social order that preceded it as modern capitalistic economies in liberal democracies are entirely controlled by a corporate derived class of merchants. Furthermore, by the end of March 2021, the only areas of the world that did not yet detect any cases of COVID-19 were the following: Africa – Saint Helena, Ascension and Tristan da Cunha; Asia – Christmas Island, Cocos (Keeling) Islands, North Korea, Turkmenistan; Europe – Svalbard; Rest of world – Cook Islands, Kiribati, Nauru, Niue, Norfolk Island, Palau, Pitcairn Islands, Tokelau, Tonga, Tuvalu (World Health Organization, 2021b). At this point in time, detected cases around the world had been on a consecutive uptrend, with 3.8 million cases having been reported in the last week of March. The distribution of detected cases around the world was as follows: 44% in the Americas; 35% in Europe; 12% in South-East Asia; 6% in the Eastern Mediterranean; 2% in Africa; 1% in the Western Pacific (World Health Organization, 2021b). By March 22, 2021 in the Czech Republic, the government declared that people could go on trips to nature or exercise on the territory of their entire district, albeit with respiratory coverings. These regulations stayed in place until May of 2021 when most retail chains and restaurants were able to open their doors (the latter were allowed to serve customers in outdoor seating areas).

By May 10, individuals were no longer required to wear masks outdoors if they kept distance of two meters away from the nearest person. On May 17, 2021, individuals could now consume meals and drinks in public areas, which marked the end of more than a year of such a restriction being in place. Up to 50 persons could also attend different organized events such as in clubs, sports, dancehalls, etc. Botanical gardens and zoos were partially reopened on May 24 and could host visitors as long as they did not overstep 50% of their venue's capacity. This is the exact point in time wherein vaccinations became accessible to the majority of the public – by June 2021, aforementioned vaccine brands made their way into nearly all regions of the world. In Europe and North America, this resulted in the next metamorphosis of digital tracking and app-based surveillance.

The Fourth Wave, May 2021-September 2021

From the height of the first wave up until the start of the third wave (May 2021), smartphone-based applications were used by governments and state security institutions to monitor individuals who were infected with COVID-19 as confirmed by formal laboratory testing and mandatory testing requirements (the most common of which were "PCR" – Polymerase chain reaction tests). School attendance was rotating on a weekly basis. On May 18, individuals who sought to exercise outside could do so without wearing a mask. Six days later, in person learning opened for students in higher education institutions via weekly class rotation. Into the beginning of summer, on June 8, authorities relaxed restrictions on the number of people that can attend events indoor (1000 persons maximum) and outdoor (2000 persons maximum) and based these new relaxed restrictions on a rule that became hegemonic for the rest of 2021 – proof of a negative COVID-19 test (ranging from antigen to PCR) or proof of vaccination or both. Additionally, on June 8, masks were no longer required for students and teachers during lessons or lectures and in workplace contexts if a given worker was not exclusively in presence of another co-worker. By July 1, outdoor venues could function at 75% of their capacity.

On July 9, many liberal democracies in the Northern Hemisphere had already administered vaccines to most of their adult populations (in terms of individuals that did want to get vaccinated, voluntarily), and here is where the following policy arose. Individuals who got vaccinated would obtain a legal "infection free status" 14 days after completing their vaccination.

By this point in time, the amount of regulations and the frequency of their changes were so extensive that one would have to devote a substantial portion of his/her day to understand the regulatory guidelines surrounding the pandemic. Different parameters of regulations and restrictions were changing very often according to specific categories of people. For example, a particular detail that was attributed to the July 9 stipulation on unvaccinated persons returning from abroad was stated as follows: "employees will not be able to be admitted to the workplace without proving a negative test. In the case of return from low- and medium-risk countries, it will be possible to attend employment until proven by a negative test, but these employees will be required to wear at least FFP2 respirators in the workplace" (Government of the Czech Republic, 2020c). At the time of these rules being initiated, I had travelled throughout different Central European states (Austria, Czech Republic, Hungary) and it was incredibly difficult to understand the different regulatory guidelines that were issued in each country because although they would be issued in a very similar (and in many instances, identical) point of time, the statuses of whether a country was a low or medium risk country would frequently change on a weekly (and in many cases, daily) basis.

On July 23, organizers of mass events were declared to have to notify regional hygiene stations "no later than 5 days before the start of the event." The latter turned out to be the last change to COVID-19 restrictions until November 15 which resulted in social interactions and human behavior across a major portion of the entire year of 2021 being technocratically regulated through QR codes, geolocation tracking, and mask mandates. The next change in regulations arose in the fifth and final wave of the pandemic.

The Fifth Wave, September 2021-December 2021

On November 15, 2021 changes to visit health and social care facilities were made and resulted in a tightening of parameters of negative COVID-19 (PCR or antigen tests) that a person had to present to enter premises. On November 22, ski resorts saw greater restrictions enforced with operators having to check validity of individuals' vaccination certificate, recovery certificate, or negative COVID-19 test when both selling tickets or during entry to a given ski lift. Likewise, on November 22, antigen tests no longer were recognized which entailed a new status quo – individuals would have to present a vaccination certificate, a recovery certificate, or a negative PCR test. By November 26, a new state of emergency was declared. All catering establishments, bars, casinos, etc., were ordered to close from 10 pm to 4:59 am. Plans for Christmas markets were also shutdown, and once again, the government reduced the number of participants in leisure activities (described as "various club, sports, cultural, dance, traditional and similar events and celebrations") from 1000 to 100 individuals maximum. Next, on December 14 greater specifications were put forward on PCR testing for students and staff across the school system. On December 30, specifications were put forward on public establishments which included shopping areas, malls, music, dance, and other forms of activities were now to be regulated through the measure of not letting in "more people into the establishment than there are seats inside" (Government of the Czech Republic, 2020c).

A new QR code and vaccination certificate application was launched by the Ministry of Health in the first days of the new year and was called, "čTečka" – which was mandated to be used by employees throughout all public venues (ranging from movie theaters to restaurants) to monitor customers' vaccination statuses. If an individual had a valid or up to date vaccination certificate (which was logged into the system via QR code), then he/she would present the certificate upon entering a given venue – the QR code would be scanned by an employee of the establishment and a green check mark would arise if the person's vaccination status was deemed valid. This type of QR-code based system was implemented widely across liberal democratic contexts. Into January of 2022, testing requirements became widely adopted across workplaces and institutions of higher education throughout the Czech Republic and other EU states. By February 15, 2020, the Ministry of Health declared that individuals' vaccine certificate validity would span to 270 days after their vaccination. By this point in time however, the severity of the virus was markedly lower as the omicron strain was prevalent, numerous vaccine doses had already been distributed throughout society, and at-risk groups had multiple vaccination doses. Numerous states in the sample of cases under attention in this book opened their borders for travelers and tourists regardless of individuals' vaccination statuses.

Above all, and this brings us to perhaps the most significant dynamic that arose with QR-code usage during the pandemic. With vaccination came numerous types of digital health certificates. The names of each certificate for the respective countries under attention are listed in the following table:

Table 4.3: Health Certificates for COVID-19

Country	Name of COVID-19 Health Certificate
Austria	Green Pass
Belgium	Covid Safe Ticket
Brazil	Não Consta
Bulgaria	COVID-19 Digital Certificate
Canada	ArriveCAN
Croatia	EU Digital COVID Certificate
Cyprus	SafePass Cyprus
Czech Republic	COVID pass
Denmark	Coronapas
Estonia	COVID-19 vaccination certificate
Finland	COVID-19 vaccination certificate
France	Pass Sanitaire
Germany	Digitaler Impfnachweis
Greece	COVID Free GR Passport
Hungary	Immunity Certificate
Iceland	COVID-19 vaccination certificate
Ireland	EU Digital COVID Certificate
Israel	Green Pass
Italy	Green Pass
Jamaica	JamCOVID
Japan	COVID-19 vaccination certificate
Latvia	COVID-19 vaccination certificate
Lithuania	COVID-19 vaccination certificate
Malta	COVID-19 vaccination certificate
Mexico	COVID-19 vaccination certificate
Netherlands	CoronaCheck App
Norway	COVID-19 vaccination certificate
Poland	COVID-19 vaccination certificate
Portugal	EU Digital COVID Certificate
Romania	COVID-19 vaccination certificate
Slovak Republic	COVID-19 vaccination pass
Slovenia	COVID-19 vaccination certificate
South Korea	COVID-19 vaccination certificate
Spain	EU Digital COVID Certificate
Sweden	COVID-19 vaccination certificate

Table 4.3: Health Certificates for COVID-19 *(Continued)*

Country	Name of COVID-19 Health Certificate
Switzerland	COVID-19 vaccination certificate
United Kingdom	NHS COVID Pass
United States	COVID-19 vaccination record
Argentina	COVID-19 vaccination certificate
Australia	COVID-19 digital certificate
Barbados	Travel Authorization
Chile	Pasaporte Sanitario
Cape Verde	Health Control Form
Costa Rica	Health Pass
Ghana	COVID-19 vaccination certificate
New Zealand	COVID-19 vaccination certificate
Panama	Check-Mig
Peru	COVID-19 vaccination certificate
Senegal	COVID-19 vaccination certificate
South Africa	COVID-19 vaccination certificate
Taiwan	Digital Proof of Vaccination
Trinidad and Tobago	T Travel Pass
Uruguay	COVID-19 vaccination certificate
Paraguay	COVID-19 vaccination certificate

The year 2021 saw by far the most frequent usage of these certificates and empirically, they were used for different purposes which ranged from travel regulations to governmental regulation of micro-level social interactions across villages, towns, cities, and social venues in communities. While not all countries issued a QR code system (e. g., the US), QR codes were nevertheless widespread. The most common manifestation of the usage of these health certificates was via the QR code which was required for individuals to present when travelling regionally or across borders, in domestic contexts and social venues which included movie theaters, restaurants, gyms, among numerous other places.

An aspect of these restrictions that readers may find to be surprising pertains to public support for surveillance in the context of the pandemic. In early 2023, results of a survey that was carried out in January of 2022 by the Heartland Institute at Rasmussen Reports on 1,016 Democrat party voters in the US revealed that more than half (55 %) of respondents supported fines against individuals who failed to get vaccinated. Nearly half (48 %) supported imprisonment for individuals that questioned the nature of vaccines on social media. What's more, close to half (45 %) of respondents voiced support for a hypothetical government program that would have temporarily placed unvaccinated individuals and their families into camps. In terms of surveillance, again, nearly half (47 %) supported state-led tracking programs to monitor unvaccinated individuals. Lastly, close to a third (29 %) of respondents believed that the state should remove parents' custody over their children if they were not vaccinated. When taken together with Republican voters who were surveyed, most of these results do indeed indicate that a majority (or more) of all respondents opposed the different topics that they were surveyed on, yet nevertheless, a particular sub-set of society who did support surveillance and authoritarian detention and restriction strategies elucidate a critical dynamic that is inherent to human nature.

In detail, these different characteristics reveal something that I believe is intrinsic to human nature and society. Regardless of the size of society it seems that othering and antagonization are clearly a part of the way that human beings perceive each others' identities. Those who suffered the heinous physical and visual ailments of leprosy were valiantly expelled from city centers and from collective participation in social circles throughout Ancient Israeli and early Roman history as did those who were experiencing symptoms of the bubonic plague in Europe. This chapter has revealed how the height of the COVID-19 pandemic led to similar outcomes across most liberal democratic polities.

Conclusion

This chapter has carried out an in-depth inquiry into five waves of the COVID-19 pandemic and has traced the different technological methodologies that states relied on in attempt to prevent, regulate, and optimize a virus that spread rampantly throughout the entire year of 2020 and most of 2021. In comparison to pandemics of the past, the COVID-19 pandemic experienced by far the most technocratic response the world has ever seen – beginning with countries that were situated close to its origin who took on comparatively harsh means to attempt to curb the virus, then as the virus made way into Europe and North America, liberal democracies exhibited illiberal behavior as supranational institutions created templates for policies that were premised on surveillance, lockdowns, and restrictions on civil liberties. As the pandemic progressed from its first to second wave, the virus mutated and eventually, vaccinations were rolled out – this took place in a time that was full of immense public angst, uncertainty, and contingency. Populations across most liberal democratic states were entrenched into technological and digital reality.

WHO's cumulative tracking estimates on COVID-19 Fatalities (World Health Organization, 2023b), while the latter are drawn from the New York Times' COVID Vaccine Tracker – a set of data that were actively tracked until March 2023 – a point in time when most countries stopped tracking the status of vaccination of their citizens (Holder, 2023).

These data can help readers contextualize a set of factors that made up a huge part of public and governmental discourse on the pandemic throughout nearly the entirety of its duration. These data are visualized below (with aid of Stata 13).

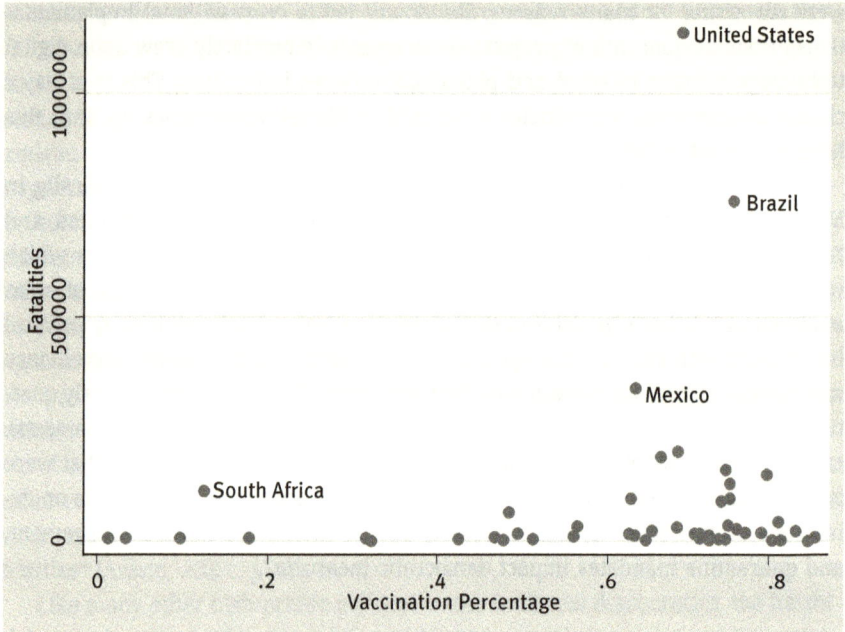

Figure 5.1: Pandemic Characteristics (n=54)

This figure clearly reveals that more Americans died from COVID-19 than in any other country in the sample of cases. Likewise, the US is a complete outlier with relation to other countries that had as much percentage of their adult population vaccinated. The other two outliers are Brazil and Mexico – both of which had similar vaccination rates as the US, but less total fatalities (albeit they do have lower populations). Levels of economic inequality and adult obesity are comparatively high in these countries. Another interesting finding here is that there is variance inherent to the extent to which populations received vaccinations from COVID-19.

Soft Laws and States of Emergencies

One of the key tendencies associated with how policies were implemented to combat the pandemic was that the most significant of restrictions such as quarantines, stay-at-home orders, restrictions on movement, travel, economic activity, and social gatherings and interactions nearly all were articulated during states of emergencies. Apart from Sweden and Taiwan, all other countries in the sample enacted states of emergencies, most of which arose in March 2020. This information is displayed in Table 5.1 – data are drawn from the European Center for Not-for-Profit Law's COVID-19 Civic Freedom Tracker (2023).

Table 5.1: States of Emergencies (n=54)

Country	State of Emergency	Month / Year
Austria	Yes	Mar-20
Belgium	Yes	Mar-20
Brazil	Yes	Feb-20
Bulgaria	Yes	Mar-20
Canada	Yes	Mar-20
Croatia	Yes	Mar-20
Cyprus	Yes	Mar-20
Czech Republic	Yes	Mar-20
Denmark	Yes	Mar-20
Estonia	Yes	Mar-20
Finland	Yes	Mar-20
France	Yes	Mar-20
Germany	Yes	Mar-20
Greece	Yes	Mar-20
Hungary	Yes	Mar-20
Iceland	Yes	Mar-20
Ireland	Yes	Mar-20
Israel	Yes	Mar-20
Italy	Yes	Jan-20
Jamaica	Yes	Apr-20
Japan	Yes	Apr-20
Latvia	Yes	Mar-20
Lithuania	Yes	Mar-20
Malta	Yes	Mar-20
Mexico	Yes	Mar-20
Netherlands	Yes	Mar-20
Norway	Yes	Mar-20
Poland	Yes	Mar-20
Portugal	Yes	Mar-20
Romania	Yes	Mar-20

Table 5.1: States of Emergencies (n=54) *(Continued)*

Country	State of Emergency	Month / Year
Slovak Republic	Yes	Mar-20
Slovenia	Yes	Mar-20
South Korea	Yes	Mar-20
Spain	Yes	Mar-20
Sweden	No	None
Switzerland	Yes	Mar-20
United Kingdom	Yes	Mar-20
United States	Yes	Mar-20
Argentina	Yes	Mar-20
Australia	Yes	Mar-20
Barbados	Yes	Mar-20
Chile	Yes	Mar-20
Cape Verde	Yes	Mar-20
Costa Rica	Yes	Mar-20
Ghana	Yes	Mar-20
New Zealand	Yes	Mar-20
Panama	Yes	Mar-20
Peru	Yes	Mar-20
Senegal	Yes	Mar-20
South Africa	Yes	Mar-20
Taiwan	No	None
Trinidad and Tobago	Yes	Mar-20
Uruguay	Yes	Mar-20
Paraguay	Yes	Mar-20

This table verifies a bold tendency by revealing that pandemic policies were, from their outset, articulated during a period of government-declared crisis. In response to the pandemic, nearly all states in the sample of cases under subsequently extended their states of emergencies in a fashion that resembled classical authoritarian modes of governance. Throughout these turbulent processes, the first and second waves of the pandemic were driven by a lack of parliamentary deliberation in most countries. Emergency health councils were appointed and epidemiologists along with politicians forged restrictions based on recommendations of the WHO and in the EU context, by the EU Commission. The manner in which all of this transpired was both rapid and multifaceted. A surprising driving force of pandemic policies pertains to a relatively vague form of law making known as the soft law. Such laws can get passed absent of consultation of checks and balances and all relevant institutional bodies. During states of emergencies, governments (especially those in the EU), enacted soft laws which then were implemented rapid pace and often were reactive in nature (Boschetti & POLI, 2021, p. 24). Legal scholars describe this form of governance as follows:

> soft law is not only omnipresent, it also operates in a composite and highly flexible web of international, supranational, domestic, and sub-state players, both public and private. It cuts across different legal systems (both vertically and horizontally) at all stages of the regulatory processes, allowing for highly flexible and direct forms of communication and dialogue across the international order on the one hand, and between individuals and businesses on the other. The complexity of the soft law web—the number of players and levels involved, and their interaction—depends on many country-specific factors (Boschetti & POLI, 2021, p. 27).

In simpler terms, soft laws are not legally binding, but do have actual empirical effects on governance and policies. Often, they can be utilized based on voluntary exchanges between different policy makers across state-level, regional, and local governance institutions. They can also be used to come to agreements with businesses and NGOs on a variety of different topics and concerns. Throughout the pandemic, especially at the height of the first wave, hundreds of soft laws were passed throughout the countries under attention in order to create wide reaching restrictions on human behavior and social interactions. These laws were not voluntarily. They were created at higher levels of government administration and channeled downwards – eventually ending up in local institutional policy domains. A common interpretation that was prevalent before the start of the pandemic was that soft laws were both encouraging and voluntary – such policy making was based on spurring cooperation, rather than coercion and intimidation. The latter, however, became predominant as COVID-19 spread throughout societies across 2020 and 2021. Soft laws were created by central governments and then passed down governmental chains of command, ending up in local contexts. Soft laws were even used in China, a context in which such forms of law making are not the norm. Cheng's (2021) inquiry into soft laws in China during the pandemic revealed how many COVID-19 measures that were enforced actually stemmed to the usage of soft laws which even though were not legally binding, still resulted in effective adoptions of emergency decrees.

In their introduction to a special issue on law making during the pandemic, Eliantonio, Korkea-Aho, & Vaughan (2021) note that, "much of the regulation of COVID-19 has taken place through circulars, instructions, guidance and other soft law norms, the legal status of which is not entirely clear." It is also noted that as tools that were utilized during the pandemic, soft laws varied according to different cultures, were carried out alongside "shady" procedures and "uncertain perceptions." Hundreds (if not thousands) of different types of soft laws were issued in countries such as Spain, Greece, Italy, and others. Some states issued soft laws for the first time (e.g., Finland), while others such as Spain or Hungary had a relatively stable history of carrying out particular public policies in such ways. Two of the key points raised in Eliantaonio, Korkea-Aho, & Vaughan's (2021) special issue on soft laws (which at the time of writing this book, features the most comprehensive scholarly inquiry into pandemic soft laws) are as follows: first, soft law measures were, in some countries, adopted in informal ways, were not subject to official scrutiny, and simply published on websites of public administration institutions. Second, throughout different jurisdictions in countries such as England, Finland, or Hungary, identifying what soft laws had been enforced was difficult for researchers because they had trouble finding information about where these laws originated from and how they were articulated.

In terms of the outlier and a country that took a highly liberal (rather than authoritarian liberal) approach to the pandemic, Sweden's lax set of tactics were based on recommendations rather than restrictions and were premised on the belief of herd immunity. In order to accomplish this, Sweden implemented few soft laws amongst its decentralized multi-level governance model which it based on personal responsibility (Winblad, Swenning, & Spangler, 2022, p. 51). This model set limits to what the national government could do and was premised on mutual trust between it and regions. This led to expert agencies gaining a high degree of independence which enabled them to interact with a decentralized health and social care system. Sweden did not end up enforcing as harsh as restrictions as many other EU countries, such as the Czech Republic for example. In March 2020, Sweden did issue restrictions, but unlike other EU countries, it did so in a manner that did not infringe on civil liberties. These restrictions were also aimed not at individuals, but at organizations (Winblad, Swenning, & Spangler, 2022, p. 52). By June of 2020, significant amendments were made that eased limitations on social interactions and even repealed a recommendation "to avoid unnecessary travel within Sweden" which was replaced to the recommendation to avoid public modes of transport. Such outcomes, nevertheless, were uncommon when viewed across the cross-national scale of countries under attention in this book. In numerous Latin American states, court-executive relations became rift with contradictions as a result of pandemic measures (Lllanos & Weber, 2023).

In terms of justifying emergency decrees and lockdowns, a report put out in late 2022 by the European Parliament's special committee on the *COVID-19 pandemic: lessons learned and recommendations for the future (COVI)*, addressed the issue of restrictions on civil liberties in a very particular way. EU policy makers framed restrictive measures as a "tool" that was "available to member states to slow the spread of an infectious disease" (Grogan, 2022, p. 8), and while admitting that, "they inevitably have significant negative social and economic costs, particularly for the most vulnerable groups in society, and by their nature have significant implications for fundamental rights" in the report, policy makers still hold onto the belief that such restrictions were to protect "rights to live, health and other freedoms." Such freedoms are framed as being "indivisible and interdependent" (Grogan, 2022, p. 8). This reflects an interesting authoritarian liberal dynamic which is fundamentally contradictory. Policy makers' motivations were driven by protecting civilians' right to life and health, but at the same time, policy makers admit that a "one-size-fits-all" approach is "unlikely to be effective" in "encouraging vaccine acceptance and tackling vaccine hesitancy" (Grogan, 2022, p. 9). It is thus unclear what the rationale for placing entire populations on lockdown was to "protect human life" when a great deal of post pandemic data point to the bold fact that societal wide restrictions did not prevent the spread of COVID-19 (more on this will be provided in subsequent chapters of this book).

Importantly, our concern here is not in whether or not restrictions should or should not have been instilled, but rather, the key is in *how restrictions were enforced* and what role democratic institutions played throughout these processes. As noted in Klepp et al's., (2022) an epidemiological inquiry into Nordic states' excess mortality rates, Sweden experienced greater mortality in 2020 than other Nordic countries (Norway, Finland, Denmark, Iceland), but less in 2021, which the authors note suggests either mortality displacement, immunity effects, or other underexplored reasons. The mean COVID-19 induced fatality age in Nordic countries was 83 years (Björkman, 2023).

Across the EU context, "civil society was also rarely involved with government decision-making, or (with some exceptions) national responses" (Grogan, 2022, p. 28). This was especially true early on in the pandemic where special counsels and advisory boards were set up in nearly all states that experienced the pandemic, and such boards were filled with health experts, epidemiologists, and other relevant people who were frequently changed and taken out of their position with no oversight or checks and balances from other institutional bodies. The enforcement of restrictive measures in France were associated with abuse of police force; in Cyprus, restrictive measures were enforced in a discriminative manner towards migrants and refugees, civilians with intellectual disabilities, and to children; in Romania, disproportionately large fines for violating restrictions were imposed as was the case in Poland (Grogan, 2022, pp. 49–50).

What's more, because of the sheer physical impact of restrictions and lockdowns, parliaments across the EU did not engage in in legislative review to sufficient extent, even if parliaments themselves were technically operational. Apart from Austria, Czech, Estonian, and German parliaments, Grogan (2022) identifies that all other EU parliaments lacked in regular scheduling of legislative review and did not attribute adequate scrutiny to pandemic measures. Less than one half of EU parliaments failed to carry out regularly scheduled debates on COVID-19 procedures and restrictions. Furthermore, Pervou (2022) argues that the pandemic affected what were once ordinary law-making processes by spurring a "new normal" in which legal dependence on science came to forefront. Not only were the total amount of laws and the frequency with which they were passed unprecedented, legislation was put forward not via collective deliberation from different bodies that have constitutionally vested legislative powers, but through executive-led actions (Pervou, 2022, p. 3). These actions manifested through special counsels in which public health officials were appointed by executive actors, who then made recommendations to enact hundreds of soft laws that subsequently were adopted across different stratospheres of governance. Such processes were widespread and as noted by Pervou (2022), "The respective legal norms that curtail civil liberties for the sake of public health and the pandemic's deceleration are by definition doubtful if not problematic" (Pervou, 2022, p. 3). Throughout these processes, a hierarchical reclassification of norms emerged – in which soft law provisions on public health became "obligatory overnight" (Pervous, 2022, p. 4).

Many of these provisions were enforced through surveillance technology. Locking down, monitoring, and tracking entire populations throughout liberal democratic states would not have been possible without the pre-existing surveillance capitalistic infrastructure. During the onset of the pandemic and its first wave, in April 2020 the EU Commission put out a report titled "epidemiological surveillance, monitoring, early warning of, and combating serious cross-border threats to health" (European Commission, 2020). The aim was to establish EU-level coordination with member states. Representatives from European telecommunication firms including Vodafone, Telefonica, Telecom Italia, Telenor, Telia, and A1 Telekom held meetings with the EU Commission to coordinate "measures tracking the spread of the virus" (Chee, 2020). This led to the establishment of an "eHealth Network" which was subsequently used to create tracking apps which functioned through Google and Apple programming interfaces on smartphones (Blasimme, Ferretti, & Vayena, 2021). Such applications gave governments not only the power, but the ability to effectively gather "metrics data for public health surveillance, such as the day, time, and duration of a contact; whether the infected user is asymptomatic; the 1st day of illness; and the date of testing" (Blasimme, Ferretti, & Vayena, 2021). Dynamics of this sort formed a significant part of the authoritarian liberal response to the pandemic and importantly, they were complimented by the usage of soft laws. What's more, they were not endogenic to the first wave of the pandemic. Later waves saw the synthesis between state security institutions and surveillance capitalistic technologies and platforms evolve.

Democracy Measures Across 54 Polities

In this section we will explore whether or not formal measures of democracy that are used throughout social science can capture abrupt changes in liberal democratic status quos that arose in 2020, 2021, and the beginning of 2022. Gauging the extent or severity of restrictions across all countries under attention in the sample of cases is a difficult task because of time and space. Waves of the pandemic, while generally applicable to all cases under attention, had different "spikes" of cases of COVID-19 infections and different strains of the virus arose at different points in time and in geographic regions of the world. Nevertheless, since the five waves of the pandemic brought about variant forms of illiberal practices, one could plausibly expect that democracy rankings would severely drop for each of the countries under attention (apart from less than a handful) for the entirety of 2020 and 2021. States shut down entire economic sectors, schools, universities, small to medium sized businesses, and restricted individuals from gathering outside.

The first set of data that we will explore are drawn from the Economist's Intelligence Unit's Democracy rankings. Here, five different categories used to create a Democracy Index – including Electoral Process and Pluralism; Functioning of Government; Political Participation; Political Culture; Civil Liberties. When these characteristics are coded by the makers of the dataset, each individual category gets assigned a score ranging from 0 to 10 (10 is the highest). Electoral Process and Pluralism measures the transparency and fairness of elections, while Functioning of Government assesses the effectiveness of the government in implementing policies. Political Participation evaluates the level of citizen engagement in the political process, while Political Culture looks at the degree of acceptance and participation in the democratic process. Finally, Civil Liberties measures the extent to which citizens are able to exercise their rights and freedoms. The scores for each category are then combined to produce an overall index score for each country.

Table 5.2: Economist Intelligence Unit Democracy Data

Country	2022	2021	2020	2019
Austria	8.71	8.9	8.96	9.09
Belgium	7.64	7.51	7.51	7.64
Brazil	6.78	6.86	6.92	6.86
Bulgaria	6.53	6.64	6.71	7.03
Canada	8.88	8.87	9.24	9.22
Croatia	6.5	6.5	6.5	6.57
Cyprus	7.38	7.43	7.56	7.59
Czech Republic	7.97	7.74	7.67	7.69
Denmark	9.28	9.09	9.15	9.22

Table 5.2: Economist Intelligence Unit Democracy Data *(Continued)*

Country	2022	2021	2020	2019
Estonia	7.96	7.84	7.84	7.9
Finland	9.29	9.27	9.2	9.25
France	8.07	7.99	7.99	8.12
Germany	8.8	8.67	8.67	8.68
Greece	7.97	7.56	7.39	7.43
Hungary	6.64	6.5	6.56	6.63
Iceland	9.52	9.18	9.37	9.58
Ireland	9.13	9	9.05	9.24
Israel	7.93	7.97	7.84	7.86
Italy	7.69	7.68	7.74	7.52
Jamaica	7.13	7.13	7.13	6.96
Japan	8.33	8.15	8.13	7.99
Latvia	7.37	7.31	7.24	7.49
Lithuania	7.31	7.18	7.13	7.5
Malta	7.7	7.57	7.68	7.95
Mexico	5.25	5.57	6.07	6.09
Netherlands	9	8.88	8.96	9.01
Norway	9.81	9.75	9.81	9.87
Poland	7.04	6.8	6.85	6.62
Portugal	7.95	7.82	7.9	8.03
Romania	6.45	6.43	6.4	6.49
Slovak Republic	7.07	7.03	6.97	7.17
Slovenia	7.75	7.54	7.54	7.5
South Korea	8.03	8.16	8.01	8
Spain	8.03	8.16	8.01	8
Sweden	9.39	9.26	9.26	9.39
Switzerland	9.14	8.9	8.83	9.03
United Kingdom	8.28	8.1	8.54	8.52
United States	7.85	7.85	7.92	7.96
Argentina	6.85	6.81	6.95	7.02
Australia	8.71	8.9	8.96	9.09
Barbados	MV	MV	MV	MV
Chile	8.22	7.92	8.28	8.08
Cape Verde	7.65	7.65	7.65	7.78
Costa Rica	8.29	8.07	8.16	8.13
Ghana	6.43	6.5	6.5	6.63
New Zealand	9.61	9.37	9.25	9.26
Panama	6.91	6.85	7.18	7.05
Peru	5.92	6.09	6.53	6.6
Senegal	5.72	5.53	5.67	5.81
South Africa	7.05	7.05	7.05	7.24
Taiwan	8.99	8.99	8.94	7.73
Trinidad and Tobago	7.16	7.16	7.16	7.16

Table 5.2: Economist Intelligence Unit Democracy Data *(Continued)*

Country	2022	2021	2020	2019
Uruguay	8.91	8.85	8.61	8.38
Paraguay	5.89	5.86	6.18	6.24
Mean	7.80	7.74	7.79	7.82

These data reveal that there was no significant change in democracy rankings as observed throughout the 54 countries under attention in this sample. While 2020 and 2021 did experience a drop, the extent of this drop was marginal. Considering that states of emergencies were enacted in nearly every single country in the sample and that entire populations were put on lockdown for months (and in some countries, years) on end, it is indeed surprising that democracy scores did not falter down several points in the rankings shown above. What's more, numerous countries in the sample even utilized pandemic restrictions to offset and repel protests and civil public gatherings which arguably constitutes among the most significant of types of authoritarian forms of social control. In Senegal, the government passed a state of emergency along with numerous decrees from the period of March to May 2020 at a time when protests erupted against the incumbent government and pandemic restrictions. In response, the government banned not only protests, but public gatherings. Executive powers were drawn upon to further restrict movement and what's more, the incumbent government also withdrew from the International Covenant on Civil and Political Rights. Up until the pandemic, the country's state of emergency could only be enacted for up to 12 days, yet through the executive issuing Decree No. 2020–830 no specification was provided on how long the state of emergency would last. Article 69 of the Senegal Constitution provides that a state of emergency may be decreed by the President for a period of 12 days, yet similar to dozens of other countries in the sample under attention, the state of emergency was extended for much longer – the executive then issued Decree no. 2020–13 to prolong the state of emergency three more months which was followed by several other decrees of similar nature (Article 19, 2021)

Although Senegal's democracy ranking did drop in 2020 and 2021, the decrease was marginal. As subsequent sections of this analysis will reveal, the drop was even less pronounced in V-Dem and Freedom House datasets. Moreover, in South Africa, similar steps were taken as in Senegal and may other countries in the sample. During the first national level lockdown (which was enacted on March 27, 2020), freedom of movement and assembly became forbidden. These measures, argue Singh & Tembo (2022), were disproportionate and violated both constitutional and human rights principles. This was especially palpable in the physical response of the state with its usage of the South African National Defence

Force (SANDF) throughout the country which Sing & Tembo (2022) argue led to brutality against civilians and brought memories of Apartheid back. Similar to Senegal, executive led action attempted to prevent protests from forming. Shifting over to the other side of the Southern hemisphere, countries in South America were observed to have enacted similar responses to the pandemic. In Chile, numerous reports of military and police-led brutalities against curfew violators emerged in late 2020. According to the US State Department, Chilean military patrols that were deployed during the state of emergency tortured upwards of five civilians that were detained as a result of the pandemic curfew – the individuals were driven to a forest and beaten (U.S. State Department, 2021). Trinidad and Tobago, in contrast, did not enact a state of emergency nor did it significantly restrict civil liberties. Its response has notably been ranked number one out of all countries in the world in the Oxford COVID-19 Government Response Tracker (OxCGRT). The country took what scholars refer to as an "all-of government" approach that was based on evidence-informed decision making and cooperative collaboration with different state institutions that had links to civil society groups (Hunt, et al., 2020).

Next, we now turn to V-Dem data. In comparison to the previous dataset, V-Dem has much more of a scholarly reach and is currently among the most discussed and cited datasets on democracy in social science. Data are coded using expert judgments drawn from a pool of over 3,700 country experts (Marquardt, 2023). Data are coded based on a 0 to 1 scale [0 represents the absence of a certain attribute of democracy, and 1 represents its full presence]. Here, 5 different categories go into the overall democracy measure including: electoral characteristics; liberal characteristics; participatory characteristics; deliberative characteristics; egalitarian characteristics. This is where very fine-tuned components of the data come in, as there exist 34 sub-dimensions and indicators.

Table 5.3: V-Dem Data 2019–2022

Country	2019	2020	2021	2022
Austria	0.837	0.836	0.837	0.841
Belgium	0.767	0.772	0.769	0.769
Brazil	0.497	0.49	0.481	0.479
Bulgaria	0.673	0.676	0.68	0.687
Canada	0.913	0.913	0.913	0.916
Croatia	0.718	0.719	0.719	0.721
Cyprus	0.739	0.738	0.738	0.736
Czech Republic	0.789	0.791	0.793	0.794
Denmark	0.917	0.916	0.916	0.918
Estonia	0.839	0.84	0.84	0.842

Table 5.3: V-Dem Data 2019–2022 *(Continued)*

Country	2019	2020	2021	2022
Finland	0.904	0.905	0.903	0.903
France	0.81	0.811	0.81	0.813
Germany	0.86	0.859	0.858	0.861
Greece	0.678	0.679	0.68	0.683
Hungary	0.55	0.553	0.551	0.551
Iceland	0.93	0.931	0.931	0.932
Ireland	0.874	0.874	0.875	0.879
Israel	0.707	0.7	0.693	0.692
Italy	0.761	0.762	0.765	0.769
Jamaica	0.744	0.745	0.745	0.745
Japan	0.811	0.811	0.808	0.808
Latvia	0.78	0.783	0.783	0.786
Lithuania	0.793	0.794	0.795	0.797
Malta	0.738	0.74	0.743	0.746
Mexico	0.65	0.646	0.641	0.637
Netherlands	0.901	0.902	0.902	0.904
Norway	0.934	0.934	0.935	0.936
Poland	0.684	0.683	0.682	0.681
Portugal	0.801	0.801	0.8	0.801
Romania	0.687	0.689	0.69	0.693
Slovak Republic	0.74	0.741	0.741	0.741
Slovenia	0.811	0.811	0.811	0.813
South Korea	0.811	0.812	0.813	0.815
Spain	0.798	0.798	0.798	0.800
Sweden	0.912	0.912	0.912	0.913
Switzerland	0.912	0.913	0.913	0.915
United Kingdom	0.899	0.9	0.899	0.901
United States	0.726	0.726	0.725	0.725
Argentina	0.715	0.713	0.712	0.711
Australia	0.914	0.914	0.914	0.916
Barbados	0.757	0.758	0.761	0.762
Chile	0.756	0.757	0.757	0.758
Cape Verde	0.679	0.679	0.68	0.682
Costa Rica	0.779	0.779	0.779	0.779
Ghana	0.562	0.562	0.564	0.562
New Zealand	0.936	0.936	0.936	0.937
Panama	0.717	0.716	0.714	0.712
Peru	0.702	0.701	0.701	0.703
Senegal	0.628	0.629	0.63	0.63
South Africa	0.732	0.732	0.731	0.732
Taiwan	0.774	0.775	0.776	0.778
Trinidad and Tobago	0.779	0.779	0.781	0.782

Table 5.3: V-Dem Data 2019–2022 *(Continued)*

Country	2019	2020	2021	2022
Uruguay	0.776	0.776	0.777	0.779
Paraguay	0.680	0.681	0.680	0.679
Mean	0.773	0.773	0.773	0.774

Here again there is no major difference between 2019 and the subsequent three years, two of which were dominated by the first four waves of the pandemic. A particular surprise is the increase in democratic ranking for the country of Italy – Italy took on among the harshest lockdowns in the first wave of the pandemic. Individuals could not leave their homes, and millions were confined to only being able to stand on the balconies of their apartments for getting fresh air.

Moving onto the final of our three datasets, Freedom House data have historically been a common point of reference for democratic performance. These data are based on a coding scheme that ranges from 0 to 100 (100 being the most democratic a state can be). Criteria here are similar to the Economist Intelligence Unit's data on democracy and include: presence of civil liberties, political rights, freedom of expression, freedom of assembly, the rule of law, functionality of government institutions. In terms of the points classification system that Freedom House data are based on, there are three different categories which include: Free, Partly Free, Not Free. These classifications are based on the total number of points a given country receives. States that get ranked from 0 and 39 are Not Free; those that get ranked 40 and 59 are Partly Free; states that get ranked from 60 and 100 are Free.

Table 5.4: Freedom House Democracy Rankings 2019–2022

Country	2019	2020	2021	2022
Austria	90	89	87	87
Belgium	93	93	93	93
Brazil	66	62	58	58
Bulgaria	72	72	69	70
Canada	98	98	98	98
Croatia	75	75	74	74
Cyprus	85	85	85	85
Czech Republic	85	83	80	79
Denmark	96	96	96	96
Estonia	89	88	86	86
Finland	98	98	98	98
France	89	89	88	88

Table 5.4: Freedom House Democracy Rankings 2019–2022 *(Continued)*

Country	2019	2020	2021	2022
Germany	93	93	93	93
Greece	84	83	80	80
Hungary	64	57	53	53
Iceland	98	98	98	98
Ireland	95	95	95	95
Israel	78	75	72	72
Italy	80	80	79	79
Jamaica	77	75	74	74
Japan	90	90	90	90
Latvia	86	87	86	87
Lithuania	85	85	83	83
Malta	87	86	86	86
Mexico	63	61	60	60
Netherlands	98	98	98	98
Norway	97	97	97	97
Poland	74	73	70	70
Portugal	90	90	90	90
Romania	73	72	70	70
Slovak Republic	79	79	77	77
Slovenia	87	87	86	86
South Korea	85	83	81	81
Spain	89	88	88	88
Sweden	98	98	98	98
Switzerland	96	96	96	96
United Kingdom	93	93	93	93
United States	86	83	80	80
Argentina	77	73	70	70
Australia	98	98	98	98
Barbados	78	76	76	76
Chile	87	85	83	83
Cape Verde	76	76	75	75
Costa Rica	83	83	83	83
Ghana	76	76	76	76
New Zealand	98	98	98	98
Panama	79	78	78	78
Peru	67	65	63	63
Senegal	69	69	69	69
South Africa	77	72	69	69
Taiwan	89	88	87	87
Trinidad and Tobago	76	76	76	76
Uruguay	85	84	84	84
Paraguay	67	65	63	63

Similar to the previous two datasets, Freedom House data do not capture the plethora of illiberal practices that manifested throughout the course of the five waves of the pandemic. As such, it is likely that the formal measures used in datasets on democracy simply were not malleable enough to pick up on abrupt changes brought about by the pandemic. Another explanation can possibly be that coders' subjective beliefs that restrictions, shutdowns, quarantines, school closures, travel cancellations, etc., were justified because states of emergencies were widely launched.

Furthermore, the following table provides estimates on the total percentage of excess mortality for the year 2020 as observed across all countries in the sample. These data were drawn from the Human Mortality Database which is described as constituting the leading scientific data resource on mortality in developed countries (Human Mortality Database, 2023). The only drawback here is that estimates, at the time of writing this book, were only available for the year 2020. Nevertheless, this was the year that the most severe variants of COVID-19 were active and spreading throughout populations. Studies on the lethality of COVID-19 variants are still very much in development (as of 2023), but scientists are starting to come to general conclusions pertaining to 1) lethality and 2) infectiousness of different variants. Liu, Wei, & He (2023) investigate case fatality rate estimates based on different variants in a cross-sectional analysis and find that significant drops in fatalities occurred from the shift to Delta to Omicron variants and that differences between different subvariants of Omicron are not evident. Case fatality rates dropped over time – for reasons that Liu, Wei, & He (2023) argue was due to a mixture of vaccine induced immunity and infection induced immunity.

Table 5.5: 2020 Excess Mortality by Country

ACountry	2020 Excess Mortality
Austria	7.90%
Belgium	16.80%
Brazil	27.10%
Bulgaria	3.70%
Canada	4.80%
Croatia	6.30%
Cyprus	1.80%
Czech Republic	8.20%
Denmark	6.20%
Estonia	8.80%
Finland	3.50%
France	8.90%
Germany	5.40%

Table 5.5: 2020 Excess Mortality by Country *(Continued)*

ACountry	2020 Excess Mortality
Greece	5.20%
Hungary	12.60%
Iceland	3.40%
Ireland	13.40%
Israel	4.10%
Italy	10.20%
Jamaica	7.50%
Japan	1.60%
Latvia	10.90%
Lithuania	13.00%
Malta	3.80%
Mexico	68.20%
Netherlands	10.20%
Norway	3.10%
Poland	8.40%
Portugal	11.10%
Romania	9.10%
Slovak Republic	12.30%
Slovenia	9.80%
South Korea	0.60%
Spain	18.10%
Sweden	7.70%
Switzerland	6.50%
United Kingdom	14.90%
United States	18.80%
Argentina	18.70%
Australia	1.60%
Barbados	4.40%
Chile	15.90%
Cape Verde	5.20%
Costa Rica	7.30%
Ghana	1.30%
New Zealand	2.10%
Panama	7.60%
Peru	14.30%
Senegal	0.70%
South Africa	5.60%
Taiwan	0.10%
Trinidad and Tobago	4.90%
Uruguay	12.60%
Paraguay	8.90%
Mean	9.35%

While qualitative inquiry into each particular country's response to the pandemic in the year 2020 would be necessary to carry out in order to understand the underlying multifaceted causes of excess mortality, it is clear that COVID-19 was a very important factor that spurred these outcomes cross-nationally. In some states such as the US, excess mortality was also driven by drug overdoses, many of which were driven by the increasing prevalence of synthetic opioids. Specifically, 91,799 people died from drug overdoses in the year 2020 alone – a 28.3 per 100,000 incident rate (compared to 2019's 21.6 per 100,000) (Centers for Disease Control and Prevention, 2022). The overall mean excess mortality for the entire sample cases is 9.35%.

Conclusion

This chapter has provided among the first multifaceted inquiries into how pandemic restrictions impacted standings of liberal democracy as measured and observed through commonly used social scientific data sets on democracy. In comparison to previous research, this chapter has drawn upon three different points of reference – beginning with the Economist Intelligence Unit's data on democratic rankings, then shifting to V-Dem, then Freedom House. The results of this chapter offer new insight into how a specific trajectory of law making was utilized throughout the height of the pandemic in the form of soft laws. There are important repercussions of this for authoritarian liberalism. Although soft laws are just one portion of the authoritarian liberal response to the pandemic, they nevertheless turned out to be critical because they went largely unchallenged and enabled policies that featured surveillance technology to not only manifest, but to be widely adopted throughout state security institutions. Apart from two countries out of the 54 in the sample under attention, states of emergencies were declared in early 2020 and it was here where the combining of authoritarian liberalism and surveillance capitalism ended up fostering wide-reaching restrictions on human behavior and social interactions. These restrictions constitute a set of processes that datasets and measures on democracy are currently not suited to capture in their observations.

Chapter 6: Optimizing the Economy and Depoliticizing Publics

A crowd of people stand in front of a supermarket parking lot on a snowy morning in Central Europe. Two security guards hover around the front of the sliding glass door of the building. The doors open every so often and a customer comes out with their groceries while another customer is let in. The crowd is becoming more tense, some begin posing questions to the security guards as to why they cannot go in the store and buy essential goods. A mother with a small child sitting in her shopping cart voices her grievance as a cold wind howls nearby. The crowd grows in size as more cars pull into the parking lot and make their way over to the front of the shop. Several elderly people start chatting about how they never thought they would have to stand in a line to get groceries after the collapse of communism. Observing this scene in a suburb of Prague, Czech Republic led me into a period of deep reflection when I eventually was able to enter the store – not only were restrictions that were enforced at the height of the pandemic completely unprecedented, but they brought back shades of memories for millions of people that had to suffer from food shortages and scarcity in earlier periods of history – eras that were obviously driven by entirely different authoritarian logics and political processes, but nevertheless, albeit for different reasons, did result in significant state-led restrictions on civil liberties and personal freedom.

As I have argued thus far in this book, there is nothing necessarily authoritarian about regulating public areas during an epidemiological emergency or crisis. However, upon deeper observation and closer scrutiny, the ways in which these restrictions manifested across many liberal democratic states was through authoritarian liberal policies that were supported by surveillance capitalistic processes. This chapter will untangle the complex dynamics that enabled liberal democratic states to not only launch the most wide-reaching processes of surveillance over entire populations in their respective history, but to simultaneously optimize economic outcomes for corporate industries. This chapter will illuminate what arguably is the most prominent component and manifestation of authoritarian liberalism during the pandemic and the most under-studied. Corporate favoritism, corporate bailouts, and corporate optimization – all represent key strategies of authoritarian liberal playbook. What's more, when writing this chapter, I came across a newly published study by Han & Han (2023) in which the authors reproduced a commonly held line of argumentation in democratization research – that the link between political leaders and economic inequality is a phenomenon which is endemic to authoritarian regimes. In this chapter, we will delve into the murky waters that surround economic policy making and demonstrate that liberal democrat-

https://doi.org/10.1515/9783111345703-006

ic states are completely engulfed in authoritarian liberal policy making. This chapter will reveal how corporate sectors greatly benefited from the pandemic as did pharmaceutical corporations, and while different sets of industries were on the brink of bankruptcy, governments bailed them out which enabled them to enter the too big to fail category.

In multiple respects, authoritarian liberalism is like any other social process – it is an evolving phenomenon that adapts to conditions and changes that occur in human society. Throughout this book thus far, I have demonstrated that surveillance capitalistic structures enabled liberal democratic governments to effectively place entire populations under lockdown and coerce deviators with great efficiency. Controlling micro-level human interactions through legislation that was continuously enforced during continuously prolonged states of emergencies was only a segment of the overall authoritarian liberal response that governments engaged in during the pandemic. Another key aspect can be observed in stimulus packages, bailouts, and financial policies that governments put forward as a response to economic downturn. This response, although variant across the sample of cases under attention, was highly strategic and turned out to be effective in spurring outcomes that favored corporate and elite interests while depoliticizing political opposition and keeping threats of revolution at bay.

In conjunction with data on different economic characteristics that are observed across all countries in the sample under attention, this chapter will also utilize comparative case study methodology to analyze numerous countries' policies and programs of bailouts, rescue packages, and how aid was delivered to corporate industries. Many of these policies were implemented across the board, so to speak, and were complemented by surveillance capitalistic logics that helped to monitor, track, and coerce populations at a time of great economic and political contingency. In a detailed brief put out by Oxfam International in early 2022, the pandemic saw rich countries across the world fail to increase taxes on the richest of their citizens and while failing to do so, they privatized public goods such as vaccine science (Oxfam International, 2022). This led to an intensification of monopolization and market concentration in these spheres which was greater in just one year (2020) than in all years from 2000–15.

A factor of economic policy in authoritarian liberal scholarship which has not seen as much development or emphasis pertains to the printing of money and adding to debt. My analysis of pandemic stimulus packages and bailouts will begin here. The "debt problem" used to be much more significant for policy makers and politicians half a century ago, but today, it is simply an issue that arises during petty political discourse across a given annual period, then tends to intensify during the time in which a given government has to agree on a fiscal budget for the subsequent year. Before delving into this key dynamic, we must consider the following set of circumstances which arose during the pandemic throughout liberal democratic states. Governments printed trillions of dollars in attempt to rescue entire industries, yet they also gave financial assistance to individuals, small to medium sized business owners, and other actors in different ways across different contexts. The ultimate outcomes of these policies can be summarized as follows:

first, policy makers added more to governments' debt in the period of two fiscal years (2020 and 2021) than nearly all previous single comparable periods of economic crisis; second, some governments sent dollars to individuals through checks in the mail according different parameters, which in turn, kept political grievances from forming into significant anti-governmental movements and revolutionary ideas; third, governments spent trillions bailing out industries that suffered as a result of pandemic-induced disruptions to economic markets, leading to numerous new industries that subsequently morphed into the too big to fail category that banking and auto industries formerly were categorized in; fourth, governments articulated particular restrictions that favored large-scale shopping outlets and corporate supermarket chains which were enabled to operate along the basis of being "essential goods" suppliers, while small to medium sized businesses were ordered to shut down. This resulted in record profits, while at the same time, did not improve epidemiological outcomes.

Printing Money, Debt, and Depoliticization

Pandemic stimulus packages were obviously not only given to corporate industries, money was also given to individuals and small businesses (depending on the country context). Although such packages only formed a small percentage of the overall amount of stimulus that was projected into to socio-economic sectors, there is a very interesting authoritarian liberal dynamic that can be observed in stimulus which went directly into the pockets of consumers. The two countries in which this dynamic was most prevalent are Canada and the United States.

The latter spent $931 billion in direct payments that were made to individuals over the course of April 2020 to December 2021 via the CARES Act, the Consolidated Appropriations Act, 2021, as well as the American Rescue Plan Act of 2021. An estimated 165 million people received these payouts which is more than half of all adults living in the states. Payouts were made on April 10, 2020, December 27 2020, March 17, 2021, and July 15, 2021. Money for these payments was not available beforehand, and in order to fund this near trillion dollar program, the government issued treasury securities along with bonds which were then subsequently sold to investors (including individuals, banks, along with holders of large capital). In a neat journalistic inquiry that covered how this process unfolded in its early manifestation, Phillips (2020) put out an article titled, "How the Government Pulls Coronavirus Relief Money Out of Thin Air" and described how "once-fringe ideas in economic theory" had taken hold and enabled the government to borrow at a rate that would lead to an unlimited escalation of national debt. The CARES Act argues Phillips, "is, in many ways, the natural result of an evolution that began with the 2008 financial crisis. Bond-buying programs that central banks undertook around the world helped ensure low-cost financing for governments running giant deficits as policymakers contended with a deep recession and a prolonged period of lackluster growth. And despite constant, high-decibel warnings that such an approach would surely ignite a surge of inflation, "it never happened" (Phillips, 2020).

In Canada over the course of 2020–21, the following stimulus packages were given to individuals: the Canada Emergency Response Benefit – which gave 82.3 billion Canadian dollars to individuals who lost employment as a result of the pandemic; the Canada Emergency Wage Subsidy – which allocated 110.6 billion Canadian dollars to employers for the purpose of giving their employees relief; the Canada Recovery Benefit – which allocated 13.1 billion Canadian to individuals who held no eligibility for employment insurance. Lastly, the Canadian government also passed the Canada Recovery Caregiving Benefit – which allocated 4.9 billion Canadian dollars to child caring adults who could not work because of having to stay with their children. By sending checks in the mail, these governments were able to keep potential grievances at bay at the height of the pandemic.

Of the two national-level movements that did arise in each of these respective countries, one numbered in the tens of millions (Black Lives Matter has been estimated to have reached 15–26 million total participants nationwide in the summer of 2020) (Buchanan, Bui, & Patel, 2020; Anisin, 2023), while the other numbered less than 50,000, the "Freedom Convoy" Canadian trucker protest which was aimed at vaccine mandates. Both movements were policy-based and were not revolutionary in their aims. In a quantitative inquiry on protest frequency during 2020 featuring 27 different countries, van der Zwet et al. (2022) observed the greatest frequency of protests from June 1, 2020 to July 1, 2020 – the number of protest events per day during this period far surpassed all other periods in the noted time frame. Apart from this contingent time period, there were sporadic anti-COVID protests that arose throughout many of the liberal democracies that make up the sample analyzed in this book. To the best of my knowledge, none of these protests resulted in regime transition or revolution. There is a clear-cut authoritarian-liberal logic behind governments' decisions to send individuals stimulus checks in the mail. In sending such checks, governments drew from their fiscal budget (and added to public debt), but did so in a very calculated manner as they ended up satisfying a majority of their populace's grievances, while at the same time, they rescued entire industries through some of the largest bailouts in economic history.

Before turning to data on bailouts, a final point must be made pertaining the aforementioned authoritarian liberal dynamic. Pandemic stimulus packages and bailouts highlight a new evolutionary turn in the authoritarian liberal playbook – since governments throughout liberal democracies have figured out how to spend billions upon billions of dollars without getting held directly accountable for the public debt that they add to, there is a new evolutionary tendency at play here which is premised on the unforetold hacking of the national debt. Electoral mechanisms that have historically been espoused as being necessary conditions for the universal functionality of liberal democracy have been sidestepped as political classes have taken their turns in positions of power but have not been accountable to voters when it comes to one of the most important elements of public policy – that of responsible fiscal policy and national debt.

As one political party's candidate gets elected and another one follows afterwards, discourse can intensify and political rhetoric can take shape that puts blame on one individual, a political party, or group of actors, but antecedent processes of adding to debt have endured onward. Table 6.1 provides information on each country's Gini-Coefficient which captures the degree of inequality in each society (data are relevant as of 2022). The lower the value for a country's Gini-Coefficient, the greater the level of economic equality. The table also lists each countries national debt as a percentage of GDP. These data are drawn from the World Bank.

Table 6.1: Inequality and National Debt

Country	Gini Coefficient	National Debt (% of GDP)
Austria	27.5	84.6
Belgium	25.9	108.2
Brazil	53.9	89.7
Bulgaria	38.3	22.6
Canada	33.7	89.7
Croatia	29.8	75.3
Cyprus	31.8	120.7
Czech Republic	24.9	34.2
Denmark	27.5	33.5
Estonia	33	8.5
Finland	26.8	60
France	29.3	97
Germany	31.7	59.8
Greece	33.6	176.2
Hungary	27.2	79.2
Iceland	24.6	38.5
Ireland	31	59.1
Israel	42.8	60.7

Table 6.1: Inequality and National Debt *(Continued)*

Country	Gini Coefficient	National Debt (% of GDP)
Italy	35.9	158.9
Jamaica	35.2	105.7
Japan	35	237.1
Latvia	35.1	38.4
Lithuania	35.7	49.1
Malta	28	44.8
Mexico	45.4	54.7
Netherlands	26.1	62.3
Norway	27.6	35.9
Poland	30.8	54.4
Portugal	32.6	118.9
Romania	35.9	37.3
Slovakia	25.4	47.2
Slovenia	25.8	72.6
South Korea	31.6	44.1
Spain	34.5	117.1
Sweden	26.8	38.1
Switzerland	29.5	41.9
United Kingdom	32.5	101.2
United States	41.4	108.1
Argentina	42.9	86.4
Australia	34.4	41
Barbados	40.9	128.8
Chile	44.4	24.8
Cape Verde	50.5	116.6
Costa Rica	48.5	60.3
Ghana	42.8	70.7
New Zealand	37.9	30
Panama	51.1	44.1
Peru	41.5	27.5
Senegal	44.6	49.1
South Africa	63	63.3
Taiwan	33.6	34.3
Trinidad and Tobago	40.3	70.5
Uruguay	39.5	60
Paraguay	50.7	23
Mean	35.7	**70.2 %**

Most importantly, as evident in the mean governmental debt per GDP (70.2 %) liberal democracies are plagued by debt problems which means governments have repeatedly spent more than is available and have surpassed any plausible status of fiscal responsibility. While doing so, governments have printed more and more money, which fundamentally will get paid for by the burdens of publics. Tax payers bare the greatest burdens when it comes to national debt as tax increases that are put forward in the future will always hit the average worker and consumer hardest. Depending on how government debt is accumulated, attempts at paying it back either transpire through increased inflation or through higher interest rates.

A Tricky but Effective Authoritarian Liberal Logic

As mentioned in the third chapter of this book, authoritarian liberal logics intensified and came to light during the 2007–8 global recession. Numerous bailouts were carried out in favor of specific industries which elucidates how policy makers have learned they can "rescue" the economy and by doing so, corporate industries obtain incredible benefits under the pretext of saving the economy and preventing it from collapse. This is made possible through very complex mechanisms and processes that are multifaceted. In the US context, elected officials – in conjunction with bureaucrats and policy makers, have continuously added to the national debt and have not been penalized by voters. Inflation-adjusted estimates put out by the Bureau of Labor Statistics indicate that national debt increased from $408 billion in 1922 to $30.93 trillion in 2022. This profound increase occurred through several trajectories which began in the 1980s. The national debt steadily increased beginning in the 1980s but then sky-rocketed into the 2000s. It grew from $12.44 trillion in 2006 to $18.43 trillion in 2010. From 2010 to 2022, it subsequently increased to $30.93 trillion.

What this profound increase means is that empirically, policy makers and elected officials have been able to add to national debt without baring the costs of public pressure and revolutionary upheaval. In terms of the pandemic period, the increase that occurred from 2019–2022 in the observed context was made possible, in part, by offsetting dissent through sending stimulus checks to hundreds of millions of individuals through the mail. Their money subsequently was spent at corporate outlets which were classified as providers of "essential goods" by governments. What's more, as stimulus checks went into the hands of millions of consumers, inflation followed very quickly. From November 2020 to November of 2021, grocery prices increased 6.4% which reflects a historically high rate of inflation that arose along with the pandemic and the many disruptions it brought about for economic markets. The key issue here is that food producers and grocery retailers had experienced historic rises in profits, but they concurrently began to profit off of inflation by rising food prices (Kelloway, 2022).

Printing money and adding to national debt is just one side to this complex array of authoritarian liberal processes. One must also consider the profound decreases in tax rates that corporations and economic elites have enjoyed since the end of the 1970s. Although there has been a very interesting and diverse history of Federal taxation in the US (Bank, 2010), at the time of writing this book, the highest possible tax percentage in the US is maxed out at 37 % for individuals and the corporate taxation rate is 21 %.

Meanwhile, in the US context, growth in real wages has stagnated for 50 years – it is estimated that in 1970, the average family income was $45,852 and by 2012 it had risen to only $51,179 (Schubert, Dye & Zeigler, 2015). In the intervening time, the participation of women in the workforce went from 40 % to 70 %, which entails that families hardly raised their incomes, even in light of greater workforce participation. What's more, in 1970, the average minimum wage (adjusted for inflation) was $7.50 per hour then by 2014, it had increased to only $9.30 per hour. Other estimates that are based on adjustments for inflation indicate that the real value of minimum wage had a peak of $12.12 back in 1968 and has since decreased – with 2022 marking a point that economists describe as being its lowest in 66 years (Cooper et al., 2022). Moreover, meanwhile, unionization has all but died off. In 1945, more than a third (35.5 %) of the workforce were members of a union, by 2010 this number dwindled down to 11.9 % (Schubert, Dye, & Zeigler, 2015, p. 80). Pandemic bailouts and stimulus packages increased inflation and public debt and also led to the abovementioned historical low in minimum wage.

Tax Rates and Bailouts

The following table includes data on the countries under attention in this book according to their corporate tax rates (as of 2023) versus the highest individual tax rates that economically well-off individuals in each country experience. A profound similarity here can be observed in how nearly all countries in the sample of 54 states have a similar corporate tax rate. This is likely due to economic globalization and the necessity of attracting foreign direct investment as well as upkeeping high rates of GDP growth for each individual country. There is some degree of variance here – as states that are landlocked, have few natural resources, or have a lack of manufacturing capacity typically will have more attractive conditions for foreign corporations to invest and set up offices in their territorial jurisdiction. As observable in the descriptive statistical output at the bottom of the table, the average corporate tax rate is nearly twice as small as the individual income tax rate as observed in the highest tax bracket across each of the countries under attention.

Table 6.2: 2021 Corporate versus Individual Tax Rates (n=54)

Country	Corporate Tax Rate	Income Tax Rate (Highest Tax Bracket)
Austria	25%	50%
Belgium	25%	50%
Brazil	15%	27.%
Bulgaria	10%	10%
Canada	15%	33%
Croatia	18%	36%
Cyprus	12.50%	35%
Czech Republic	19%	22%
Denmark	22%	55.90%
Estonia	20%	20%
Finland	20%	31.75%
France	28%	45%
Germany	29.58%	45%
Greece	24%	44%
Hungary	9%	15%
Iceland	20%	46.24%
Ireland	12.50%	48%
Israel	23%	50%
Italy	24%	43%
Jamaica	25%	25%
Japan	30%	55.95%
Latvia	20%	31.40%
Lithuania	15%	32%
Malta	35%	35%
Mexico	30%	35%
Netherlands	25%	49.50%
Norway	22%	22%
Poland	19%	32%
Portugal	21%	48%
Romania	16%	45%
Slovak Republic	21%	25%
Slovenia	19%	50%
South Korea	25%	42%
Spain	25%	45%
Sweden	21.40%	57.1%
Switzerland	18.2%	40%
United Kingdom	19%	45%
United States	21%	37%
Argentina	30%	35%
Australia	30%	45%
Barbados	5.5%	35%
Chile	27%	35%
Cape Verde	25%	35%

Table 6.2: 2021 Corporate versus Individual Tax Rates (n=54) *(Continued)*

Country	Corporate Tax Rate	Income Tax Rate (Highest Tax Bracket)
Costa Rica	30 %	25 %
Ghana	25 %	30 %
New Zealand	28 %	33 %
Panama	25 %	25 %
Peru	29.50 %	30 %
Senegal	30 %	50 %
South Africa	28 %	45 %
Taiwan	20 %	45 %
Trinidad and Tobago	30 %	30 %
Uruguay	25 %	36 %
Paraguay	10 %	10 %
Mean	22 %	37 %

The following figure provides estimates on data on totals (in $USD) that governments spent on bailouts throughout the pandemic. These data are drawn from the COVID-19 Global Gender Response Tracker which monitored responses taken by governments on a cross-national basis through triangulation of data drawn from the Data Futures Platform (a project of United Nations Development Program) (COVID-19 Global Gender Response Tracker, 2023). Here, characteristics of data originated from the World Bank and WHO, and upwards of 1,000 observations on economic, financial, and fiscal support for businesses and entrepreneurs were analyzed. The figure was produced via the R programming language (R 4.3.0).

For the sake of clarity, these data are visualized in billions rather than trillions – as there is great variance inherent to the size of countries' economies. The US, for example, spent an estimated 5.3 trillion USD on bailouts, while a small country like Malta spent 400 million. Although not entirely visible in Figure 6.1, readers must keep in mind that every single country in the sample spent a significant amount of money on bailouts and stimulus packages. The only two states that spent less than 1 billion were Malta and Trinidad and Tobago. While individuals in countries that did send out individual stimulus checks likely were somewhat happy or supportive of getting money from their government due to lockdowns and restrictions, little did they know that the money they earn would be worth less in the future as debt would sky rocket, inflation would increase, and they would, down the line, end up paying much more on goods than the value of their stimulus because of tax increases. Above all, as subsequent sections will demonstrate, in numerous states, stimulus checks were sent out at a time that was marked by corporate retailers being classified and regulated as the only valid suppliers of "essential goods." Before turning to providers of essential goods, attention must be paid to

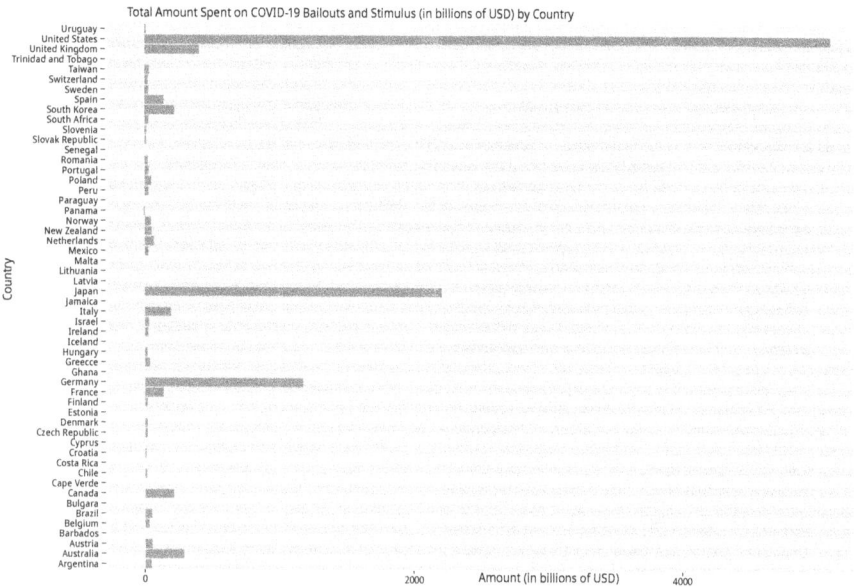

Figure 6.1: Bailouts and Stimulus (n=54).

the aviation and transport industries as these sectors represent the first major set of corporate interests that were hit by pandemic travel restrictions that ensued during the first wave.

The Aviation and Transport Industries

The first set of industries that were immediately impacted by border shutdowns and the cancellation of cross-border travel were airlines. Similar to how the automotive industry in 2007–8 were deemed "too big to fail" – the airline industry during the height of the pandemic was no different. At the height of the first wave of the pandemic, in March 2020, the US Senate voted unanimously (96–0) on a $58 billion rescue package for the aviation industry in America (Shepardson & Rucinski, 2020). Furthermore, airline industries were faced with what Lee (2021) accurately summarizes as an unprecedented set of challenges at the start of the pandemic that constituted an existential threat. The types of financial support that governments provided airline industries began in early 2020 and are categorized by Lee (2021) in the following ways: (i) loans and loan guarantees, (ii) equity acquisitions, (iii) hybrids (a mix of debt and equity financing), (iv) wage subsidies, and (v) flight subsidies. Additionally, other financial measures include tax exemptions, deferments, and waivers of airport-based charges (Lee, 2021).

> The following governments provided bailouts to their airline industries (drawn from Lee, 2021, Table 1. "Government-backed loans and guarantees"):
> Austria – Austrian Airlines (150 million euro loan)
> Belgium – Brussels Airlines (287 million euro loan)
> Denmark – SAS Airlines (137 million euro loan)
> Netherlands – Air France/KLM (2.4 billion euro loan)
> Estonia – Nordica (8 million euro loan)
> Finland – Finnair (600 million euro loan)
> France – Air France/KLM (7 billion euro loan)
> Germany – Condor (550 million euro loan)
> New Zealand – Air New Zealand ($580 million loan)
> Norway – Norwegian Airlines (277 million euro loan)
> Portugal – Tap Air Portugal (1.2 billion euro loan)
> Romania – Blue Air (62 million euro loan)
> Spain – Iberia (750 million euro loan); Vueling Airlines (260 million euro loan)
> Switzerland – Edelweiss and Swiss Airlines (1.4 billion euro loan)
> United Kingdom – EasyJet (690 million euro loan); Ryanair (670 million euro loan); Wizz Air (344 million euro loan); IAG-British Airways (2.21 billion euro loan)
> United States – $25 billion for various airlines; $4 billion for cargo air carriers.

In total, these figures reveal the extent to which governments who headed liberal democratic polities helped save an entire industry. Saving airlines however, was not only done through providing direct loans, but governments engaged in equity acquisitions. The following states gave hundreds of millions of euros or dollars to airlines through the following equity programs. Data below are drawn from Lee (2021) and include the total amount of money that was spent (Lee, 2021, p. 713):

> Finnish Government – Finnair (286 million euros for shares)
> German Government – Lufthansa Group (300 million for shares, 20% stake)
> Israeli Government – El Al ($34 million for newly issued shares)
> Latvian government – Air Baltic (250 million euros for 10.95% of shares)
> Portuguese government – Tap Portugal (55 million for shares, 22.5% stake)
> Singaporean government – Singapore Airlines ($986 million for shares)
> Swedish and Danish governments – Scandinavian Airlines (194 million euros for new shares; 292 million euros in equity participation; 22% stake)

What's more, Lee (2021) identifies "hybrid financing" that was carried out by governments. Here, governments spent a substantial amount of money on different forms of debt conversion including bonds and loans. For example, the German government gave the country's historical flagship airline, Lufthansa, 1 billion euros as a part of a convertible debt package. The New Zealand state gave Air New Zealand a loan of NZ 900 million with an option to obtain repayment through raising capital after 6 months of conversion of the loan to equity (Lee, 2021, p. 714). Some governments, such as the Danish or US governments, gave what Lee (2021) describes as "flight" subsidies to airlines in which networks of support were created to airlines to cover airport fees and charges (such as those arising from flight cancellations or planes with empty passengers). At the time of writing the noted article, Lee (2021) argued that governments faced a difficult set of questions surrounding how to "maintain fair competition in moments of heightened nationalization" (Lee, 2021, p. 719). Lee contends that since governments were under pressure to shield airlines from competition that they had a specific stake in equity in, this would pose risk for market-based competition.

Latin American states also engaged in similar bailouts of their airlines. For example, in Mexico, the government allocated $2.5 billion in aid to its aviation industry which was a mixture of tax relief policies, guarantees on loans, and subsidies among other actions. Brazil spent upwards of $680 million bailing out three airlines (Viga Gaier & Rochabrun, 2020).

In terms of automotive industries, by November 2020, the German government had already allocated over 5 billion euros to its auto sector. The move was made in part to provide a financial boost for the struggling industry within Germany and its exports, and likewise to pump over a billion into subsidies for electric vehicles (DW News, 2020a). This particular bailout exemplifies the authoritarian liberal logic that was at play in governments' fiscal policies during the height of the pandemic. Since masses of people were ordered to stay at home, the total number of time people spent traveling on all forms of transport declined. For example, one estimate puts 2020's total decline at 73 fewer hours spent in traffic, sitting in cars for Americans, 26 for Germans, and 37 for the British (Gitlin, 2021). Pumping billions into automotive industry was done by the German government to support what journalists referred to as an "ailing" industry, while on the other hand, the government literally sought to optimize the industry itself. Steffen Seibert (who at the time was Angela Merkel's main spokesman) designated the aim of the bailout package to foster "long-term structural change" in the industry (DW News, 2020a). Prior to bailout itself, in September 2020, Merkel's government met with representatives of the auto industry and at the time, journalists described the purpose of these meetings to "look in to possible ways of strengthening the equity capital of companies in the sector, especially for suppliers" (Reuters, 2020b).

This bailout was likely inspired by events that arose just a few months earlier in May 2020 in France where the French President, Emmanuel Macron, put forward an 8 billion euro plan for France's automotive industry. This stimulus package was described by Macron as not only being a saviour, but as a transformative force, "We need to not only save the industry but transform it" (DW News, 2020b).

These are clear examples of how bailouts were used in times of economic crisis to optimize large economic sectors. The French example is particularly interesting because Renault, the French auto conglomerate, received an estimated 5 billion euros out of the 8 billion state package and Macron declared that this aspect of funding was contingent on the conglomerate keeping two of its large production plants in France open (DW News, 2020b). If we take a glance back to October 2008 – the height of the global recession and near market collapse, a $700 billion bailout was passed by US Congress then signed by President G.W. Bush in order to "revive car loans and help create a mass market for electric vehicles" (Crawley, 2008). In a very familiar set of public statements, the spokesperson of General Motors Corporation (Greg Martin) stated that, "We believe this bill will restore confidence in our financial markets and restore the flow of credit that in our business dealerships so heavily depend on" (Crawley, 2008).

It is important to note that some countries in the sample of cases had governments which took variant means to bail out industries such as Mexico whose left-wing President, López Obrador spent more on tax relief, social programs, and promoted decreases in interest rates for small businesses to be able to take out loans from banks. At the height of the pandemic, journalists described the Mexican president's actions as follows, "López Obrador has rejected bailouts, tax breaks and debt relief, making Mexico the only large country in the Western Hemisphere that has not announced an economic stimulus package to counter the economic fallout from the pandemic" (Linthicum, 2020).

Ultimately, across most countries in the sample under attention, tax payers bared the brunt of the burden of bailouts. This is observable in two realms – the first being public debt, and the second in the direct ways that specific corporations dealt with stimuli they received from governments. In the US context, it is estimated that over $50 billion that airlines received from the state in workers' subsidies ended up being utilized by airlines, but not for the support of their workforce. In detail, $50 billion in taxpayer money was given to airlines, but they then did not contribute the money to furlough which resulted in severe work shortages and hundreds of flight cancellations (Laris & Aratani, 2021). Along with some airlines (such as Delta Air Lines) who gave bonuses to managers, tax payer money was allocated to rescue companies. This is a clear authoritarian liberal set of policies that is not only akin to aviation industries. In a non-authoritarian liberal "free market" the clear course of action that would need to be taken by governments would be to let corporations go through bankruptcy processes which would then logically be followed with new actors purchasing their assets and filling industry voids.

Empirically, we can begin to observe repetitive cycles in which corporate industry losses get accommodated by the state through taxpayer money in times of economic crisis. In contrast, during periods of growth and economic stability, corporations self-privatize their profits, raise prices for consumer items and services, and provide bonuses to top management and shareholders that can number up in the tens of billions. As previous authoritarian liberal led interventions in history have shown us, it is clear that incumbent governments will go to great lengths during periods of economic or political crises in order to optimize economic outcomes. It appears that most liberal democratic governments heavily favored state-led economic restructuring of their economies during the pandemic – a dynamic that also can be observed in a different industry, consumer shopping.

Empirical Analysis of Corporate Super Markets

We now turn to what arguably is the most significant of policies that exemplify authoritarian liberal-led optimization of the economy attuned to corporate preferences – the super market. In contrast to bailouts of transport industries, the following sets of regulations that were put forward by many governments were directly linked to surveillance technologies and interestingly enough, the development of different restrictions and regulations manifested in different waves of the pandemic. Throughout most of 2020 and 2021, state health institutions dictated that all restaurants, small shops, and other shopping establishments must close. This left only large-scale supermarkets (nearly all of which are owned by corporate chains) to be left open. Large supermarkets were referred to as "essential businesses" – stores that sold goods on a mass scale.

Such designations had significant repercussions for commerce and exchange across entire economies. It is estimated that supermarkets ended up distributing 98 % of their net profits to shareholders through both share buybacks and dividends (Oxfam International, 2021). Supermarket chains such as Ahold Delhaize, ASDA, Costco, Lidl, Rewe, Walmart, Morrisons, Jumbo, Sainsbury's, Tesco, and numerous others experienced significant jumps in their retail sales from the second to fourth quarter of 2020 (11.1 %) which far surpasses the 1.6 % growth they experienced in the same period during 2019 (Oxfam International, 2021, p. 5). The shares of these retailers saw a profound historical increase in which their capitalization increased by $101 billion from just March to December of 2020. In this vein, the historical profits reaped through pandemic-based advantages saw CEOs and top management of these corporate chains giving out large increases in dividends to shareholders.

These outcomes did not arise out of thin air – they were specifically driven by pandemic policies which led to the shutting of small and medium businesses. Corporate chains however, were left open and were the only focal points of where individuals could obtain "essential goods" for large portions of the pandemic. According to the noted Oxfam report, more than 60 different new billionaires were created directly because of the corporate food and shopping industry during the pandemic. The following corporate entities experienced increases in sales growth which range from a minimum of three-fold to a maximum eight-fold growth: Ahold Delhaize; Albertsons; Costco; Kroger; Walmart; Morrisons; Sainsbury's; Tesco. It is estimated that private entities such as the German conglomerates Aldi and Rewe experienced similar rates in sales growth. By the tail end of 2020, observers and industry experts were already starting to catch on that the corporate retail store was doing much better than usual. As noted by Redman (2020), "Conventional supermarkets benefited as food shopping occasions that might have included multiple trips – perhaps to a warehouse club, mass merchant, discount grocer, specialty retailer and/or dollar store – were consolidated into a visit to the neighborhood grocery store" (Redman, 2020).

As I argued in Anisin (2022a), for some odd reason, policy makers believed that coercing individuals to only shop in one designated area (the corporate retail store) would lead to a lesser likelihood of the virus spreading. Empirically, at least from my own experience being in different EU countries there were more people, on average, in supermarket chains than I had ever seen because there simply was no other way or place to get goods from. Pandemic restrictions also led to a profound transformation in how people shopped with e-commerce (electronic based shopping) which has been observed to have increased by estimates of at least 50 % in developed countries (McKinsey & Company, 2022). On-demand delivery grocery shopping blossomed and became much more of an accepted phenomenon during the pandemic (Gupta, 2022). Specifically, delivery services were widely utilized during lockdowns, and once again, the only approved companies and businesses that could legally stay open tended to be corporate supermarket retailers as these types of businesses not only had pre-existent infrastructure, but also capital to invest in the expansion of such services.

The concentration of resources that many of these retail conglomerates enjoy must also be given attention. As noted by Stephens (2022) in an inquiry on the context of Canada, supply chain concentrations came to the forefront during the pandemic – conglomerate Cargill experienced record profits in 2022 and these profits were so significant that individuals from the company's ownership board (the Cargill family) ended up being classified into the Bloomberg Billionaires list. What's more, by 2022, inflation in Canada reached a height that had not been seen since 1991, and the average grocery food bill increased by an estimated 70 % from the year 2000 to 2000, while median incomes did not keep pace. Corporate retailers, notes Stephens (2022), enjoy concentrated food systems and supply chains and experienced record profits – a process Stephens classifies as "greedflation." Greedflation entails that corporate concentration of resources (such as food and essential goods) leads actors to jack up prices to unnatural levels during periods of crisis.

These dynamics are obviously very akin to authoritarian liberalism, especially as observed in the context of the pandemic. It is estimated that consumers spend one out of every three dollars at the American conglomerate, Walmart (Foodandwaterwatch, 2021). What's more, since the 1990s, it is estimated that the rise of supermarket chains (and their associated "supercenters") resulted in a 30% decrease in the number of grocery stores across the United States. This is a fundamental change when compared to status quos of consumer behavior that were prevalent decades ago. In the 1980s, local and regional retailers were much more prevalent. Into present day, conglomerates began to dominate and the combined market share of the four largest retailers in the U.S. (Walmart; Kroger; Costco; Albertson) tripled from 23% in 1993 to 69% in 2019 (Foodandwaterwatch, 2021). These companies have struck numerous deals with producers of food brands such as Kraft Heinz, General Mills, Del Monte, PepsiCo, etc., to dominate the market through providing attractive prices on products including some of which are sold exclusively within a given supermarket chain. Simultaneously, this has resulted in higher prices at smaller outlets and an existing state of affairs that would not be far-fetched to classify as an oligopoly. Historically recent mergers between producers such as Kraft and Heinz further exacerbate these conditions. Within these corporate structures of production and exchange, specific companies dominate the production, importation, and exchange of entire products such as beer; bottled water; carbonated soft drinks; coffee; bread, among many other products.

In the British context, similar dynamics can be observed as conglomerates such as Tesco, Morrisons, ASDA, and others hold a disproportionate amount of the market share. These conglomerates hold upwards of 80% of the supply chain. The following data indicate publicly declared profits of each of these companies: Tesco – 2020, reported £551 million; 2021, £825 million. Sainsbury's – 2020, reported £255 million; 2021 – Sainsbury's £356 million. Asda – 2020, £584 million. Morrisons – 2020, reported £431 million. Aldi U.K. – 2020, £271 million ($375 million).

QR Codes and Surveillance

Consumers relied on purchasing essential goods from shopping outlets that were permitted to be open under pandemic regulations. By the time vaccines were widely available for adult populations, the creation of digital health certificates during the pandemic enabled individual data to be synthesized into national and cross-national health security architecture to track billions of peoples of health statuses and biological parameters. Most commonly health certificates were utilized by individuals, businesses, and state security institutions through QR codes which would typically be held via a PDF in a given person's smartphone, then would be scanned by another smartphone that was connected to the internet and verified according to a given set of regulatory characteristics that were determined by a given country's ministry of health. The certificate would necessarily show if a person had an "up-to-date" vaccination status (usually less than 6 months old), had tested negative for the virus (in a formal outlet sanctioned by a given state), or had logged a formal "recovery" from the virus (also logged into a formal outlet sanctioned by a given state). In some liberal democratic contexts such as Australia, QR code check-in regulations were widely required for hospitality venues and indoor premises (Davies et al., 2023). QR codes were used for contact tracing – when an individual would have their QR code on their smartphone scanned by a given employee of a store or public venue, they then would be directed to a mobile application or website where they would have to fill in their details – the application, note Davies et al., (2023), was designed by the government and monitored. Similar regulations were enforced throughout 2021 and early 2022 in Germany – where individuals would have to not only present a valid QR code to enter a museum and other similar venues, but would then have to fill out their details either electronically or on paper (at the said venue) upon entry into its premises.

Readers may wonder, how did the synthesis between surveillance capitalistic structures and authoritarian liberal governmental behaviors actually occur, in real-time, during the pandemic? In previous chapters, I described that surveillance capitalism had been increasing in prominence prior to the onset of the pandemic. It was not until the pandemic, however, that these two phenomena merged and synthesized. March 2020 appears to the exact month that this occurred – when the development of surveillance frameworks was deliberated upon by the US government and its "active talks" that occurred between representatives of Facebook, Google, and what journalists at the time described as a "wide array of tech companies" (Romm, Dwoskin, & Timberg, 2020). The way that these processes were portrayed at the time was through an idea of anonymous public health data tracking that would be used to help stop the spread of the virus.

Events and interactions that arose in March 2020 signify how a wide spectrum of individuals and groups' positions on technology were clearly aligned with the belief that it could be used to slow down the spread of a virus. What's more, it is debatable if a given respiratory illness (such as any of the coronaviruses) can be stopped at all.

QR codes on specific health statuses of individuals became prominent alongside other technologically influenced processes such as geo-location tracing. In August 2021, like dozens of other governments, the French government began to require individuals to show a QR code to enter restaurants, cafes, and to travel by plane, bus, or train (Corbet, 2021). The code would indicate if a person had an up-to-date vaccination (6 months old or newer) or if they had proof of a negative test. The French Transport Minister, Jean-Baptiste Djebbari, stated that, "We're going to enforce massive controls" (Corbet, 2021). As late as January 2022, some countries still had "non-essential" stores shut while corporate retail outlets functioned. In the Netherlands, an association of non-essential goods stores made pleas to the government on January 14, 2022 that they were willing to do whatever necessary if they could just open their doors to customers, "associates are willing to do whatever is necessary – checking for proof of vaccination, making masks mandatory inside or only allowing a limited number of customers per square metre – if it means they can reopen" (Raker, 2021).

In September 2021 the whole Ontario region of Canada required proof of COVID-19 vaccination to from entering "non-essential businesses" which included gyms, restaurants, movie theaters, and concert halls among other venues (Katawazi, 2021). The profound nature of this restriction was that it directly prevented individuals who were either not vaccinated or who did not have a negative COVID-19 test enter non-essential businesses. Next, in October 2021, Bulgaria issued a "green certificate" that became mandatory for individuals to present and get scanned if they were to enter restaurants, cinemas, gyms and shopping malls (Reuters, 2021). The logic that underpinned this decision was similar to other countries' health institutions and policy makers – Bulgarian Health Minister Stoicho Katsarov's justification was that, "The number of new infections and deaths is rising. That forces us to impose additional measures. All activities indoors should be carried out with a green certificate" (Reuters, 2021). Indeed, not all countries in the sample required individuals to present their vaccination status to enter social venues (e. g., Poland or Sweden), and some countries had variant regulations with regard to vaccination status in which they permitted individuals to enter all places that sold d without showing proof of vaccination, while restricting them in other contexts such as movie theaters and in sports halls (e. g., Lithuania).

A key takeaway point here is that at the height of the pandemic (in the first and second waves), shops and services were closed apart from corporate retailers that were classified as sole providers of "essential goods." Subsequently, into the third wave, as noted, with the rolling out of mass vaccination, technological architecture drawn from surveillance capitalistic platforms was widely drawn upon to regulate human behavior on a scale hitherto unimaginable. This elucidates how the synthesis between authoritarian liberalism with surveillance capitalism unfolded empirically across some of the countries under attention.

In a different vein, the policy to instill QR code requirements via the presentation of digital health certificates for all social venues apart from corporate providers of essential goods was premised on a clear position of moral authority. This explicates a protruding characteristic of the pandemic response in liberal democracies as a whole. Specifically, many decisions to restrict, regulate, and manipulate human behavior and social interactions were done on a moral basis – especially in public hygiene wherein those who did not adhere to mask wearing guidelines or did not get vaccinated were ostracized as either murderers or criminals in the most extreme of examples. In November 2021, Pfizer's CEO, Albert Bourla, stated that opponents to vaccines are "criminals" which costed "millions of lives" – "They're not bad people. They're criminals because they have literally cost millions of lives" (Lovelace Jr., 2021). It was also not uncommon to hear opinion pieces and op-eds throughout media in which threats were made on a moral basis. For example, a former long serving member of local government in Palm Springs, California argued that, "those who refuse to obtain shots when eligible should be charged with murder; if not in the first degree, then some degree thereof. And they should be deprived of any coronavirus-related relief payments," further arguing that, "as a civilized country, we hold those who commit personal injury and economic injury crimes accountable" (Gray, 2021). The highly antagonistic torrent of rhetoric that became prominent throughout English speaking countries at the height of the pandemic attached clear moral hierarchies between the "vaccinated" and "nonvaccinated," with the latter being labelled as "antivaxxers" and conspiracy theorists that were spreading misinformation (Mak, 2021). These dynamics, as noted in earlier chapters, were also prevalent across bureaucratic discourse in the European Commission.

The irony behind these antagonisms is that throughout much of the Western world, those who opposed pandemic mandates (such as mask regulations or mandatory vaccination) were typically classified as right wingers, while those who were pro-pandemic regulations were left wingers. This ultimately resulted in the "left" (broadly conceived) as being supporters of not only the pharmaceutical industry, but of industry as a whole. Moultan (2023) makes an interesting claim that big pharma has, since the late 1980s and the AIDS crisis, become intertwined in promoting humanitarian language borrowed from activist groups and has enlisted radicals for rhetorical support. Anthony Fauci was a primary actor in this context. Decision making in how the AIDS crisis was handled ended up bringing about grave consequences for gay communities due to fear campaigns. With the COVID-19 pandemic, similar mistakes were made, argues Moultan (2023) as Fauci and the public health establishment portrayed COVID-19 as a universal threat, when in reality it was a risk for those with pre-existing conditions and elderly segments of the population. Both AIDS and COVID-19 were thus propagated to "promote dependence on the public-health apparatus and expand the consumer base for novel pharmaceuticals" (Moultan, 2023).

The Lasting Authoritarian Liberal Impact of Bailouts

In total, economists estimate that $4 to 5 trillion was pumped into the American economy over the course of the pandemic and was comprised of grants, loans, and tax breaks – all of which contributed to the most "costliest economic relief effort in modern history" (Whoriskey et al., 2023). This attempt at optimizing the economy during a crisis saw economic packages given to large businesses who laid off many workers, and in turn, were granted huge tax breaks by the Federal government. For instance, the Cheesecake Factory furloughed an estimated 41,000 employees, only to gain a tax break of $50 million (Whoriskey et al., 2023). What's more, an estimated $454 billion went directly to the Federal Reserve in order to "stabilize markets" and help companies such as the banking conglomerate, Wells Fargo, the telecommunications conglomerate, AT&T, or the cruise conglomerate, Carnival to borrow money at exceedingly low rates while laying off many of their employees. Whoriskey et al. (2023) estimate of the 16% of the total $4 trillion that went to fighting the actual health crisis; $884 billion (around 1/5th) went to relief aid for workers and families; while more than a majority (estimated at $2.2 trillion) went to industry.

There are two key implications from the massive bailouts that many liberal democratic governments put forward during the pandemic. The first pertains to public debt. As in the previous major economic crisis of 2007–8, the trillions that were spent on bailing out corporate industries were never paid pack, but rather, money was drawn from a complex web of bonds, treasuries, and other similar institutional deposits that are tied to the end outcome of reckless money printing. Elected politicians signed off on legislation and stimulus packages, and as one would expect, their behavior has led some to correctly ponder if, "Is it real money that will eventually need to be paid back? Or can it somehow be left behind by one generation to be written off by the next?" (Inman, 2020). At the time of writing this book, there appears to be no clear-cut solution or any set of realistic policies that liberal democracies have put forward to deal with the pressing issue of public debt. The second key implication here pertains to the heterogeneous nature of how incumbent governments sought to optimize economic outcomes through economic restructuring and corporate favoritism. The numerous "bailouts" or "stimuli" that were put forward throughout the pandemic were not homogeneous and were technically variant according to industry and according to whether the state already had equity in a given company or if it did not.

In a different vein, it is interesting to ponder over why for some odd reason, no other infectious diseases or viruses have ever been so widely regulated by public health authorities across the world nor have they been as sensationalized by media organizations as COVID-19 was. By looking into liberal democratic governmental health regulations and recommendations that were prevalent before the pandemic, I discovered that governmental health institutions put forward vague and highly passive recommendations on vaccination for different diseases and infections. In 2013, the Center for Disease Control and Prevention's "most frequently asked questions" about vaccinations and travel included a variant amount of information and recommendations from this governmental health institution on what individuals' opportunities are according to travel destinations and different types of viruses and infectious diseases. With reference to yellow fever, the CDC advised that, "some countries in South America and Africa require you to provide proof that you have been vaccinated against yellow fever by presenting an International Certificate of Vaccination or Prophylaxis when entering the country. However, there are other popular travel destinations where the threat of infection with yellow fever virus is very real, and there is no requirement for you to be vaccinated to enter the country" (CDC, 2013).

Similar vagueness can be observed throughout the Netherlands' governmental recommendations for vaccinations that were put forward in 2017 – here, it was noted that, "To visit some countries, you need certain vaccinations. Travel vaccinations are provided by the municipal health service (GGD), vaccination clinic and some family doctors," further reading that, "However, it is important that you get personal advice. The length of your trip, the conditions under which you will be travelling, your age, health and whether you take any medication are all important factors" (Government of the Netherlands, 2017). The passivity of this language completely differs from the highly alarmist nature of COVID-19 recommendations. Subtropical regions of South America and Africa are prone to the mosquito-borne infection of yellow fever – an infection that has an estimated mortality rate of 20–50%. Not all countries in which this deadly infection can manifest however, require or enforce proof of vaccination for yellow fever. In 2011, the Norwegian Institute of Public Health's Africa travel vaccination advice page stated that, "Vaccination against various diseases is recommended when travelling to most African countries" (Norwegian Institute of Public Health, 2011). The specific word, "recommended" is much different than the "required" mandates of the COVID-19 vaccine that were common throughout the course of the pandemic.

The indistinctness and ambiguity of pre-pandemic recommendations on vaccination and the lack of strict enforcement by national-level health institutions as well as by international health institutions (such as the WHO) brought about a status quo that fundamentally differed when compared to what arose during the pandemic. These differences are epidemiologically significant because mortality rates from COVID-19 are estimated to be less than 1%, whereas numerous other infectious diseases and viruses are much more lethal. In Gautret et al.'s (2012) inquiry in the journal, *Clinical Microbiology and Infection*, it was demonstrated that cases of the poliovirus were widely identified from January 2008 to March 2011 in the following countries: Angola, Benin, Burkina Faso, Central African Republic, Chad, Côte d'Ivoire, Democratic Republic of Congo, Egypt, Ethiopia, Gabon, Ghana, Kenya, Liberia, Mali, Mauritania, Niger, Nigeria, Republic of the Congo, Senegal, Sierra Leone, Sudan, Togo, Uganda, Afghanistan, India, Kazakhstan, Nepal, Pakistan, Tajikistan, Turkmenistan, Russian Federation. Childhood immunization from this virus does not necessarily protect an individual from contracting the virus again if they are exposed to it as an adult – and despite health institutions' "recommendations" travelers from France, Germany, Australia, the US, and other countries had low vaccination coverage (Gautret et al., 2012).

The authors note that the WHO's World Health Assembly did not endorse a polio-travel vaccination requirement in 2006 and that, "until the disease has been certified as eradicated globally, the risks of acquiring polio (for travellers to infected areas), and of re-infection of polio-free areas (by travellers from infected areas) remain" (Gautret, Botelho-Nevers, Brouqui, & Parola, 2012). Similar adversities are identified by the authors with reference to the pathogen called Neisseria meningitidis serogroup W135 and measles – both of which are far more lethal than COVID-19.

Vaccines and Pharmaceutical Corporate Profits

One critical aspect of the trajectory of corporate favoritism that has been identified throughout this chapter which I did not include pertains to vaccine mandates and their relation to corporate profits. At the time of writing this book, not enough information was made available (both medical and economic) about the whether vaccine mandates overstretched their purpose and were mandated for the larger objective of spurring positive corporate profit outcomes rather than preventing outcomes that were adverse public health. With this being said, preliminary evidence is starting to emerge that population wide vaccine mandates were ill-fated to begin with. For example, in April of 2023 the US Food and Drug Administration (FDA) revealed that COVID-19 vaccines do not prevent infection nor transmission – this piece of information completely contradicted the policies and recommendations that health institutions were providing throughout the height of the pandemic. In April 2023, the FDA was pressured by a coalition called "The Coalition Advocating for Adequately Labeled Medicines" to update labels that hitherto had been placed on Pfizer and Moderna vaccines. The intent of this advocacy group was to persuade the FDA that high ranking political actors such as President Biden and Anthony Fauci had misinterpreted the basis of vaccination throughout 2020 and 2021. Specifically, in July 2021, President Biden stated the following,

"If you're vaccinated, you're not going to be hospitalized, you're not going to be in the IC unit, and you're not going to die." Additionally, Biden stated, "you're not going to get COVID if you have these vaccinations." Both statements however, are false (Woodward & Yen, 2021), and represent a misconstrued logic that policy makers widely advocated in 2021.

Throughout 2021, Anthony Fauci and similar high profile medical experts were widely arguing that vaccinated individuals are highly unlikely to transmit the virus and that vaccinated people become "dead ends" for the virus (Choi, 2021). It is plausible to assume that these particular points of argumentation were behind the widespread adoption of discriminatory practices that were instilled by governments and state security institutions against unvaccinated persons, and above all, the articulated necessity of vaccinating entire populations from COVID-19, including school children and college students. Likewise, in a feature put out by the BMJ in September 2021 titled, "Vaccinating people who have had covid-19: why doesn't natural immunity count in the US?" asked the following pertinent question, "As more US employers, local governments, and educational institutions issue vaccine mandates that make no exception for those who have had covid-19 questions remain about the science and ethics of treating this group of people as equally vulnerable to the virus – or as equally threatening to those vulnerable to covid-19 – and to what extent politics has played a role" (Block, 2021).

This feature proceeded a landmark study that was put out by the Cleveland Clinic which revealed that vaccination reduced the risk of COVID-19 for individuals that never tested positive, but was not observed for those who had already been infected previously. Specifically, the study assessed 52,238 different individuals to probe whether they had been infected with the virus according to their vaccination status and history. The study found that, "Individuals who have had SARS-CoV-2 infection are unlikely to benefit from COVID-19 vaccination, and vaccines can be safely prioritized to those who have not been infected before" (Shrestha et al., 2021). The implications of the study are that vaccination may not have been necessary to mandate for individuals who had already been infected with the virus. The fact that policy makers across liberal democratic contexts did not give serious consideration to the notion of herd or "natural" immunity should raise a red flag. The aforementioned study is not the only one of its kind – similar inquiries have since been published and have come to analogous conclusions. Pilz et al. (2022) demonstrate that natural immunity shows similar effect sizes in protecting individuals from reinfection and that natural immunity "may offer equal or greater protection against SARS-CoV-2 infections compared to individuals receiving two doses of an mRNA vaccine," and what's more, the authors recommended that, "Natural immunity should be considered for public health policy regarding SARS-CoV-2."

Conclusion

This chapter has analyzed the final piece of the authoritarian liberal response to the pandemic that took place across liberal democracies over the course of 2020, 2021, and the first portion of 2022. Stimulus packages and bailouts that governments throughout liberal democratic contexts put forward were arguably the most complex in economic history – for the first time, hundreds of millions of people received checks in the mail during an economic downturn, yet concurrently, governments gave aid to corporations that across most cases of the contexts under attention, surpassed what they gave to individuals. This chapter has identified a key dynamic in particular regulatory restrictions that were placed around consumption and the obtaining of food, water, supplies, and basic or "essential" goods. Governments widely enabled large supermarket chains to keep operating at the height of the pandemic, and used digital surveillance technologies to ensure that populations adhered to various guidelines that restricted and regulated human behavior, social interactions, commerce, and consumerism. In multiple respects, this chapter's analyses and observations are among the most important to the phenomenon of authoritarian liberalism as the pandemic has revealed that authoritarian liberal dynamics and processes have evolved with the times, and took on new, exacerbated forms that were meshed with surveillance capitalistic mechanisms. A key implication that can be drawn from this chapter's inquiry pertains to adding a deeper conceptual basis to knowledge and theory on authoritarian liberalism – it is clear that governments in liberal democratic states have learned to manipulate and change the trajectory of economic structures to the favor of elite actors and corporate industries. They also have grown to learn how to manipulate electoral mechanisms to their favor, particularly through avoiding accountability to adding to both inflation and public debt. When the economy goes south or takes a significant downturn and corporate industries are on the brink of bankruptcy, authoritarian liberal elected officials, lobbyists, economic policy makers and government bankers step in and act as artificial saviors. In part, many of these types of these policies have resulted in an interesting evolutionary dynamic – authoritarian liberalism is an evolving phenomenon that has seen different trajectories of causal operation in different periods of economic downturn. There now appear to be relatively predictable repetitive cycles in which corporate industry losses get accommodated by the state through different mechanisms in times of economic crisis. This is done through governments giving industries direct capital, providing equity programs, and even restriction of human behavior and social interactions as observable during pandemic shutdowns of non-corporate retail shopping outlets. Empirically, this has all come at the great expense of the average tax payer and at the grander expense of national debt.

Chapter 7: Conclusion

The COVID-19 pandemic was a once in a lifetime experience for many generations of people across the world, for young and old, and for rich and poor. The rapid onset of the pandemic was so profound that few comparable events can be observed in the last century of history. The pandemic impacted an already globalized and highly intertwined world and made many grasp the extent of humanity's interconnectivity. By 2023 however, it seemed as though much of the English-speaking world had moved on from the topic of COVID-19, vaccines, lockdowns, and mask mandates. The virus had mutated so many times that vaccination was only recommended to extremely vulnerable groups. Some countries, such as France, Denmark, and Switzerland, completely stopped recommending vaccines for COVID-19 to all of their population – the Swiss Federal Office for Public Health declared that most people in Switzerland had already been vaccinated or had recovered from COVID-19 and that their immune system had therefore been exposed to the virus (Schemmel, 2023).

Throughout this book, I have put forward an inquiry of the pandemic through investigating political, economic, social, and technological processes that were implemented across a sample of 54 liberal democratic states. Many of these liberal democracies took on authoritarian liberal modes of governance to deal with the pandemic and drew from surveillance capitalistic structures in attempt to prevent the spread of the virus, to contain it, and to monitor individuals' biological and health parameters. The pandemic was, to the best of my knowledge, the first globalized instance of surveillance of human beings' biological parameters and statuses. Since nearly all countries enacted states of emergencies as a result of the pandemic's onset and borders were literally closed for travel, the first wave of the pandemic created a set of crises that are unparalleled to anything I have witnessed. These crises led to the surfacing of authoritarian liberal governance across a broad array of policy schemes that ranged from bailouts, stimulus packages, to restrictions of certain types of shopping outlets, and fine-tuned monitoring of social interactions and human behavior.

Surveillance capitalistic structures and mass amounts of data that were previously owned and controlled by private technological corporations enabled many governments to effectively shut down entire populations' social interactions. As I have argued throughout this book, the synthesis between these two phenomena – authoritarian liberalism and surveillance capitalism – was significant but also variant. Not all countries in the sample (n=54) took on authoritarian liberal approaches to the pandemic and not all countries placed their populaces under heavy surveillance. Most however, did, including countries that not only makeup

https://doi.org/10.1515/9783111345703-007

some of the largest economies in the world, but more importantly, countries that are highest ranked across democracy measures. In contrast to research on democratic backsliding and populism, the argument of this book has drawn attention to a different set of illiberal tendencies which manifested during the pandemic. In doing so, it has provided a comparative set of inquiries.

This book has not taken issue with the reality that the pandemic constituted a major public health problem during its onset nor has it disputed that COVID-19 disrupted may different socio-economic structures. I have, nevertheless, argued that there were deeply rooted forces at play that gained prominence and agency throughout the pandemic and these forces enabled aforementioned restrictions, shutdowns, stay-at-home orders, school lockdowns, and state-led control of movement to effectively be implemented and extended across the time period of nearly three years. Throughout this time, governments repeatedly rescued major corporate industries and manipulated market outcomes in attempt to spur efficient results for specific groups of actors. Similar to previous economic downturns and crises, authoritarian liberal policy making came to the forefront and the logic of free market-based competition went out the window as industries became "too big to fail." Liberal democratic governments quantitatively spent hundreds of trillions on combatting the ill effects of economic downturn. At the tail end of 2020, numerous reports also estimated that the entire total of stimulus packages for COVID-19 related factors was upwards of $9 trillion in 2020 alone (Anderson, 2022).

Already in early May 2020, pandemic related disruptions were starting to impact how tens of millions of children in developing countries were obtaining immunization from deadly diseases. Routine immunization for diseases of polio, measles, and diphtheria in low-income countries decreased as estimated (by the WHO, UNICEF, and the Gavi and Sabin Vaccine Institute) to impact close to 80 million children under the age of 1 years old (World Health Organization, 2020e).

The end outcome(s) of pandemic policies that have been investigated in this book can be summarized as follows: the largest and most wide-reaching restrictions on human behavior, economic activity, and social interactions were successfully implemented with aid of surveillance capitalistic technology and data architecture; governments printed trillions of dollars to bailout corporate sectors and upkeep industrial output(s) across different sectors of economies; state security institutions successfully tracked and monitored of hundreds of millions (if not billions) of individuals' health statuses through technological platforms. Psychologically, masses of people worldwide experienced increases in anxiety and depression – in the first year of the pandemic, cross-national estimates indicate that these ailments increased 25% (World Health Organization, 2022b). Even larger increases can be observed in particular countries if viewed on a national level. Once the pandemic ended however, things went back to normal. Many of the industries that were on the brink of collapse enjoyed booms and record profits, while workers' incomes suffered from high inflation.

Above all, it appears that all of the surveillance, monitoring, restrictions, mandates, and frequent changes were ineffective in both reducing transmission of the virus and in decreasing its impact on mortality. One need only to take a comparative guise into Sweden's pandemic health outcomes versus other Nordic or EU countries.

An Unstandardized Conclusion

The conclusion of this book differs from traditional conclusions that one may come across in a social science monograph. Considering the rapid dissemination of information that currently exists in our world, a substantial number of medical inquiries and post-pandemic revelations emerged at the tail end of the pandemic, and even more were published in early 2023. The following section will reflect on some of these inquiries and relate them to restriction policies that were widely implemented during periods of state of emergencies in nearly all of the 54 countries that have been analyzed in this book. Throughout my time presenting this book (either in whole or in segments) in academic circles and seminars in its earliest draft forms, I come across a wide range of responses, most of which were overwhelmingly constructive. One particular aspect that tended to arise was always at the tail end of the presentation or during post-presentation discussions in which colleagues and interested members of the public raised questions about what could have been done differently or what I would have recommended had I worked in a given council or institution on dealing with the pandemic during the time of its occurrence.

My position was (and continues to be) that I first and foremost am not an epidemiologist, but I did closely follow the numerous policies that governments took to deal with the pandemic and the many different problems posed for populations. My response during the outbreak was the same as it is post-pandemic – specifically that population-wide lockdowns, restrictions, quarantines, vaccination mandates, and mask mandates were flawed and probably should have only been implemented in February, March, and April of 2020, if at all. The Swedish approach appears to have been among the few democratic and deliberative approaches taken throughout the 54 countries under attention in this book. The banality of many of the measures that countries adopted in the first, second, and third waves of the pandemic now increasingly appear to be nonsensical and are illustrative of either a social experiment or elite-led manipulation of entire populations. Throughout varying points of the year 2021, there were frequent changes in regulations on mask wearing which saw rules being changed from wearing masks to wearing no masks to wearing a certain type of mask to then wearing no masks again. Likewise, shifting indoor and outdoor venue capacity rules based on the total number of people allowed per m2 in a seemingly random manner now also seems to be quite an absurd way to carry out policy if we consider the fact that public transport systems in most countries in the sample remained open.

For substantial durations of time in 2020 and 2021, restaurant dining was marked by individuals having to wear masks when entering a restaurant and while going to the bathroom, but not while they were eating. Perhaps the most bizarre of the many reoccurring changes that arose throughout the year 2021, for example, can be observed in how testing requirements were altered according to guidelines that sought to monitor the validity of different types of tests and vaccination certificates. Some weeks saw stringent requirements which forced people to either provide a negative PCR test that is no older than three days old, while other weeks required individuals to only present self-bought antigen tests that were less than 24 hours old when presented. To make matters more complicated, once vaccines became available for all adults across the societies under attention in this book, testing requirements shifted back and forth from necessitating that individuals present either of the aforementioned negative test plus a vaccination certificate or QR code, or only the latter. When second rounds of vaccines were created to tackle new strains of the virus, some countries (e. g., Germany) set up even stricter rules that required individuals to present double or even triple vaccine certificates to enter shops, restaurants, and other venues.

During the second and third wave of the pandemic, Android and IOS based smartphone applications were forged by governments to monitor and regulate human behavior on a mass scale in attempt to optimize epidemiological outcomes. Data from people's geolocation(s) were monitored by the state which allowed authorities to identify whether public gatherings were taking place (potentially against restrictions) and if an infected individual left his/her place of residence. In this regard, at the height of the pandemic, there was an interplay between surveillance and restrictions which varied according to context and country. This leads one to ponder over whether if the pandemic, as observed across most liberal democracies, was simply representative of mismanaged public health policy?

What Went Wrong

Pandemic restrictions were incredibly detrimental to certain groups, while at the same time, they were beneficial to others. This observation applies to demographic outcomes as well as economic and political outcomes. Beginning with the former, it is starting to become clear that shutting down schools, enforcing mask mandates for children, along with similar restrictions appear to have played no significant role in preventing the spread of COVID-19 nor in decreasing the mortality rate that societies experienced from the virus. In both public and scholarly discourse, attention throughout the pandemic tended to be geared towards highly antagonistic discourse in which opponents of pandemic restrictions were labelled as right wing or associated with populist behavior. It appears that the opposite might have actually been what unfolded empirically. Recent meta-analyses have revealed that the foremost types of restrictions (e. g., mask wearing, school lockdowns, economic shut downs) did not actually stop the spread of the virus and what's more, Jefferson et al's. (2023) 326-page inquiry published in the Cochrane database of systematic reviews (which is close to a gold standard of scientific reviews) utilized a total of 76 randomized control trials with 610,872 participants to investigate whether mask wearing and physical interventions reduced the outcome of influenza-like illness and COVID-19. Their inquiry reveals that physical interventions (including screening at entry ports, isolation, quarantine, physical distancing, personal protection, hand hygiene, face masks, glasses, and gargling) did not end up being effective in actually preventing the transmission of respiratory viruses. The following eye-opening findings were produced by the report. First, wearing masks in a given community "makes little or no difference" to COVID-19 outcomes when compared to not wearing masks. Second, there is no clear difference between wearing an N95/P2 respirator when compared to medical/surgical masks, both of which have uncertain effects on clinical respiratory illnesses and also make little or no difference for outcomes of influenza-like illnesses.

Mask mandates generally were carried out through executive actions in which a given governing incumbent political party cooperated with ministries of health or similar state institutions to prevent the spread of a disease. More and more information about the adverse nature of pandemic restriction policies continues to reveal itself through different mediums of news reports and communication. For example, it is now known that early double blind randomized control trials that were run on Moderna and Pfizer vaccines were much more adverse than was revealed in 2020. It was only in September of 2022 when a peer reviewed study published in the leading journal, *Vaccine*, identified the risk of serious adverse events that were observed in the early trials of the COVID-19 vaccinations. During the early portion of the first wave of the pandemic, a collaboration that was endorsed by the WHO was created and implemented to observe mRNA COVID-19 vaccine trials in adults. When compared to placebo baseline values of serious adverse events arising from mRNA COVID-19 vaccines, adults who got vaccinated during trials with either Pfizer or Moderna vaccines experienced rates of 10.1 and 15.1 per 10,000 participants – which totals to the Pfizer trial exhibiting a 36 % higher risk of serious adverse events and the Moderna trial exhibiting a 6% higher risk. This combines to a 16% higher risk of serious adverse events in vaccine recipients versus placebo (Fraiman et al., 2022). The Pfizer vaccine led to a much higher number of cardiac disorders. What these results entail is that early trials had already revealed that individuals who got vaccinated were likelier to suffer adverse events from being vaccinated (including getting hospitalized from vaccination) than from contracting the COVID-19 virus.

While it is indeed true that nearly all vaccine trials always tend to reveal adverse events and symptoms (regardless of whether it is a COVID-19 vaccine or not), and that some vaccines have even been withdrawn after administration (such as the rotavirus vaccine which was withdrawn after 1 million children were vaccinated), data reveal that both the Pfizer and Moderna vaccine trials had a higher excess risk than the risk reduction of COVID-19 hospitalization relative to the placebo group with the numbers being – 15.1 per 10,000 versus 6.4 per 10,000 for Moderna and 10.1 per 10,000 versus 2.3 per 10,000 for Pfizer. The authors of the study conclude that "Full transparency of the COVID-19 vaccine clinical trial data is needed to properly evaluate these questions. Unfortunately, as we approach 2 years after release of COVID-19 vaccines, participant level data remain inaccessible" (Fraiman et al., 2022).

In July of 2022, the BMJ (British Medical Journal) which is among the top historically ranked scientific medical journals released an open letter concerning Pfizer and Moderna vaccine trials which problematized these corporations' lack of transparency with their trial data. As noted by the authors of the open letter, "To the best of our knowledge, regulators such as the European Medicines Agency, UK MHRA, and Health Canada lack electronic individual participant data (IPD) datasets" (BMJ, 2022). The letter then called for unique participant ID numbers, demographic details (age, sex, etc.), and dates pertaining to when different doses of vaccination were administered during the trials. At the time of writing this book, these data still have not been made available. Further, Kisielinski et al. (2023) carried out a meta-analysis of 2,168 studies to investigate the impact that mask wearing had on different health outcomes and perceptions of wellbeing. It was discovered that surgical masks and N95 masks had the most detrimental effect on well-being. The most significant impact was in interfering with oxygen uptake and CO_2 release – this led to mask-induced-exhaustion-syndrome which the authors argue promoted "Downstream physio-metabolic disfunctions."

While readers may find this finding to be a bit eccentric, it necessarily needs to be contextualized because there were literally entire seasons (and in some countries, a year or more) where masks were required to be worn in every single area apart from one's own home. This means that individuals' lives outside of their home were entirely lived through wearing masks, including indoors at workplaces. Mask mandates resulted in hundreds of millions of people (if not billions) having to live their life through the prism of a mask which is why fine-grained data on potential adverse side effects of wearing masks can now be observed.

Jefferson and 11 colleagues conducted a study for Cochrane, a British nonprofit that is widely considered the gold standard for its reviews of health care data. Their inquiry's conclusions were based on 78 randomized controlled trials, six of them during the Covid pandemic, with a total of 610,872 participants across multiple countries. It was found that mask mandates exhibited no protective effects against COVID-19. There are many other similar studies that have since been published. For example, a study put out by the National Bureau of Economic research in mid-2022 estimated that upwards of 97,000 excess deaths (60 per 100,000) arose in the US over the course of 2020 – 21 – deaths which were not brought about by the actual virus of COVID-19, but by the policies that were instilled upon the population by governments to attempt to stop or slow down the spread of the virus. Similar estimates were identified for the EU context (64 per 100,000), with the outlier being Sweden (33 per 100,000) (Mulligan & Arnott, 2022).

Theoretical Considerations

When it comes to combining different theoretical perspectives and frameworks, this book has demonstrated why it is not only fruitful, but analytically necessary to combine different approaches to explain large scale socio-political and economic outcomes. There are many dimensions to periods of social turbulence, to political dislocations, and to economic downturns. When regular life gets disrupted and previous status quos change over the span of a few short weeks, the contextual conditions in which different causal factors arise in and then become operative are so heterogeneous that it is very unlikely a single social scientific framework can account for outcomes that are exceedingly complex and involve interactions between domestic governmental institutions, international institutions, individuals, groups, and corporations. Indeed, much depends on the dependent variable, outcome, or set of outcomes that are being explained in a given scholarly inquiry. For instance, one of the key frameworks that have been applied to the study of social control is the Foucaultian framework of Biopolitics which has been implemented through interdisciplinary research on a range of topics to assess how political forces operate throughout public administration over large-scale societal governance outcomes. This framework emphasizes that public policies are premised on regulating human beings as a species through political administrative decision making which exemplifies what Foucault argued (originally in 1976) is "biopower" – a type of power that seeks to administer, optimize, and subject populations through control and regulation (Foucault, 2019). Biopower is not necessarily concentrated as it can function and be exercised through different networks that can be either physical or symbolic (Lazzarato, 2002). The significance of biopower pertains to one of its hidden components – that power holders will attempt to upkeep their own groups' hierarchical status through offsetting threats from other groups.

While it is indeed true that some pandemic policies were demonstrative of exercises of political power, biopolitical dynamics and biopower were clearly not the only set of dynamics that were prevalent during the pandemic. This framework tells us little about why some periods of life are marked by more or greater manifestations of biopower in comparison to others. As this book has revealed, there were many different manifestations of authoritarian liberal policy making which were carried out in different spheres of economies and benefited different actors and groups at different points in time. Above all, there is a clear variance that is inherent to pandemic responses – while most countries initiated states of emergencies and carried out widespread lockdowns, there were still some others which did not extensively shut down their entire societies for extended periods of time.

Along similar lines, bailouts and stimulus packages were widely given to corporate actors and industries to a greater extent than individuals and small to medium sized businesses, yet there were also some states (e. g., Mexico) that carried out policies which favored the latter over the former. By and large, authoritarian liberal policies favored corporate interests at the expense of working classes and middle classes.

Theoretical frameworks that are produced in social science need to be adjusted, combined, and deliberated upon with reference to the phenomena that they are seeking to explain. Often, different periods of history are marked by different causal processes and mechanisms. Seeking to generalize over vast periods of history with one single framework will lend one into either an echo-chamber or into an explanatory snare. From the outset of conceptualizing the frameworks that were used to write this book, it was clear that the pandemic brought about an immensely diverse amount of outcomes and that complex causality was inherent to most phenomena that arose, especially in public policy making and governmentality. A key example of this complexity pertains to how surveillance architecture was set up and implemented throughout liberal democratic states. Prior to the pandemic, governments did indeed possess sophisticated surveillance tools and did have a capacity to monitor individuals and groups that were threatening to political status quos. However, governments did not have the wide-reaching capacity to place their entire populations under lockdown and surveil movement of civilians based on their geolocations. This is precisely when the synthesis between surveillance capitalism and authoritarian liberalism came into play – telecommunication, internet, and other technological corporate entities' data architecture was handed over to government security institutions and entire populations were then monitored – human behavior and social interactions were regulated, at first, according to designated local areas and then once vaccination and widespread COVID-19 testing infrastructure emerged, states obtained detailed knowledge of the biological statuses of populations through databases that tracked individuals' vaccination records and illness histories. The latter were then used to classify entry parameters into most public areas and social venues throughout the countries analyzed in this book.

The Lasting Impact of Restrictions on Public Health

Scholars must cast a critical guise over political discourse that was used to justify vaccine mandates and the many different restrictions that accompanied social interactions for individuals that chose not to be vaccinated or those that had already been infected with the virus. For example, Canadian Prime Minister Justin Trudeau's statements in 2021 were very coercive, "If you've done the right thing and gotten vaccinated, you deserve the freedom to be safe from COVID," (Scherer & Gordon, 2021), or US Vice President Kamilla Harris' statement, "if you are vaccinated, you are protected" warrant critical reflection.

In 2021, Pfizer reported a 92% increase in operational growth which equated to an estimated profit of $81 billion dollars. As of 2022, the Pfizer mRNA vaccine held 70% of the entirety of US and European markets (Allen, 2022). Pfizer became the hegemon across most liberal democratic states in the Northern hemisphere and it did so with the help of governments. For instance, the US, led by the Biden administration, continuously bought hundreds of millions of doses of booster shots of Pfizer's covid vaccine – paying an estimated $30.47 per dose for the Fall 2022 season which totaled to $3.2 billion (Allen, 2022). As noted by Allen (2022), "Because the virus keeps mutating and will be around for a long time, the market for Pfizer's products won't go away. In wealthier countries, the public is likely to keep coming back for more, like diners at an all-you-can-eat restaurant, sated but never entirely satisfied." Pfizer had also donated more to political candidates in the 2020 election cycle than any other drug company, noted Allen (2022), and what's more, its partner company, BioNTech, also received an estimated $445 million from the German government.

Future research should investigate the high degree of complexity of networks of actors and groups that were involved in the pandemic response across liberal democracies – incumbent governments, lobbyists, epidemiologists, scientists, public health officials, and different corporate sectors, all of which contributed to policy outcomes (whether purposefully or inadvertently). The desire and necessary pursuing of the technocratic optimization of individuals' and populations' biological wellbeing during a public health crisis resulted in social life across most liberal democracies being controlled and monitored through technological means with few checks and balances, a lack of respect for democratic norms, and significant absence of deliberative debate on important topics such as whether children or at risk groups should be forced to wear masks for the greater part of a given day, for months (and in some instances, more than a year) on end. As I have revealed above, at the tail end of the pandemic, research on this topic revealed profoundly contradictory information with relation to pandemic policies that were widely adopted throughout the first, second, and third waves.

Concluding: The Future

An ironic, albeit disturbing characteristic of the pandemic is that it disappeared almost as fast as it emerged. At the tail end of the pandemic, a major conflict erupted between a world power (Russia) and one of its neighboring states (Ukraine) who ended up receiving hundreds of billions of dollars of military assistance from dozens of Western states and NATO – bringing the world closer to a nuclear exchange than arguably any point other than the Cuban missile crisis. This war has ended up being the largest military conflict experienced since WWII on European soil and at the time of writing this book, it will likely surpass all other military conflicts that arose in other areas of the world as well.

On a final note, it is clear that the ways in which governments restricted travel, shut down economic activity, and prevented social gatherings from taking place throughout the pandemic can indeed be used again in the future as the nature of power that contemporary states hold, especially in terms of states' security capacity, is exceedingly disproportionate. Across most countries in the sample of cases that have been analyzed in this book, governments and state institutions demonstrated that they had more than a sufficient amount of security architecture that would necessarily be needed to putatively restrict movement on a population level (for upwards of say, 90 % or more of a given population) if a given crisis or set of crises arises in the future. These characteristics and conditions signify a profound set of changes that are inherent to the way that human behavior can now be controlled and altered by government.

References

Achilli, S. J., & Edge, D. (2020). Inside Italy's Covid War. May 19, 2020. *PBS Frontline.* Retrieved from: https://www.pbs.org/wgbh/frontline/documentary/inside-italys-covid-war/

Allen, A. (2022b). How Pfizer Won the Pandemic, Reaping Outsize Profit and Influence. *KFF Health News.* July 5, 2022. Retrieved from: https://kffhealthnews.org/news/article/pfizer-pandemic-vaccine-market-paxlovid-outsize-profit-influence/

Amin, R., Sohrabi, M. R., Zali, A. R., & Hannani, K. (2022). Five consecutive epidemiological waves of COVID-19: a population-based cross-sectional study on characteristics, policies, and health outcome. *BMC Infectious Diseases,* 22(1), 1–10.

Anderson, S. (2022). WHO: Spending on Health Increased 6% in 2020; but Detailed Data Mostly Covers Rich Countries. *Health Policy Watch.* December 8, 2022. Retrieved from: https://healthpolicy-watch.news/who-finds-spending-on-health-increased-in-2020-but-sparse-dataset-leaves-many-questions-unanswered/

Andrew, J., Baker, M., & Huang, C. (2023). Data breaches in the age of surveillance capitalism: do disclosures have a new role to play? *Critical Perspectives on Accounting,* 90. https://doi.org/10.1016/j.cpa.2021.102396

Angwin, J., Savage, C., Larson, J., Moltke, H., Poitras, L., & Risen, J. (2015). AT&T Helped U.S. Spy on Internet on a Vast Scale. *The New York Times.* August, 15, 2015. Retrieved from: https://www.nytimes.com/2015/08/16/us/politics/att-helped-nsa-spy-on-an-array-of-internet-traffic.html

Anisin, A. (2023). The Perfect Storm? Political Instability and Background Checks During COVID-19. *International Journal of Criminology and Sociology,* 12, 15–26. https://doi.org/10.6000/1929-4409.2023.12.02

Anisin, A. (2022a). Pandemic surveillance capitalism: authoritarian liberalism or democratic backsliding? *Journal of Political Power,* 15(2), 262–278.

Anisin, A. (2022b). Heidegger and the Technocratic warping of the COVID-19 pandemic. *Cultural Studies ↔ Critical Methodologies,* 22(3), 321–332.

Anisin, A. (2022c). Discourse, antagonisms, and identities during the COVID-19 pandemic. *Revista Crítica de Ciências Sociais.* 128. Onlinefirst. https://doi.org/10.4000/rccs.13434

Anisin, A. (2022d). *Mechanisms and the Contingency of Social Causality.* Newcastle upon Tyne: Cambridge Scholars Publishing.

Anisin, A. (2021). The contradictions of COVID-19 and the persistence of Western Hegemony. *Politikon,* 48(2), 331–346.

Apple. (2020). Apple and Google partner on COVID-19 contact tracing technology. April 10, 2020. Retrieved from: https://www.apple.com/newsroom/2020/04/apple-and-google-partner-on-covid-19-contact-tracing-technology/

Article 19. (2021). Senegal: COVID-19 response violates rights. June 28, 2021. Retrieved from: https://www.article19.org/resources/senegal-covid-19-response-violates-rights/

Ateba, S. (2023). Dr. David Martin Claims COVID-19 Pandemic Was Pre-Meditated Domestic Terrorism, Speaks at European Parliament Summit. *Today News Africa.* May 28, 2023. Retrieved from: https://todaynewsafrica.com/video-dr-david-martin-claims-covid-19-pandemic-was-pre-meditated-domestic-terrorism-speaks-at-european-parliament-summit/

Bank, S. A. (2010). *From Sword to Shield: the Transformation of the Corporate Income tax, 1861 to Present.* Oxford: Oxford University Press.

BBC News. (2014). Edward Snowden: Leaks that exposed US spy programme. *BBC News.* January 17, 2014. Retrieved from: https://www.bbc.com/news/world-us-canada-23123964

https://doi.org/10.1515/9783111345703-008

Bermeo, N. (2016). On democratic backsliding. *Journal of Democracy*, 27(1), 5 – 19.

Bibri, S. E., & Allam, Z. (2022). The Metaverse as a virtual form of data-driven smart urbanism: On post-pandemic governance through the prism of the logic of surveillance capitalism. *Smart Cities*, 5(2), 715 – 727.

Bigo, D., Guild, E., & Kuskonmaz, E. M. (2021). Obedience in times of COVID-19 pandemics: A renewed governmentality of unease. *Global Discourse: An Interdisciplinary Journal of Current Affairs*, 11(3), 471 – 489.

Björkman, A. (2023). The Swedish COVID-19 control measures and the national commission report. *Acta Paediatrica* (Oslo, Norway: 1992), 112(1), 8.

Blasimme, A., Ferretti, A., & Vayena, E. (2021). Digital contact tracing against COVID-19 in Europe: Current features and ongoing developments. *Frontiers in Digital Health*, 3, 61.

Blavatnik School of Government. (2022). COVID-Government Response Tracker. Retrieved from: https://www.bsg.ox.ac.uk/research/research-projects/covid-19-government-response-tracker#:~:text=The%20Oxford%20Covid%2D19%20Government,taken%20to%20tackle%20COVID%2D19.

Bonefeld, W. (2017). Authoritarian liberalism: From Schmitt via ordoliberalism to the Euro. *Critical Sociology*, 43(4 – 5), 747 – 761.

Block, J. (2021). Vaccinating people who have had covid-19: why doesn't natural immunity count in the US? *BMJ*, 374. doi: https://doi.org/10.1136/bmj.n2101

BMJ. (2022). Covid-19: Researchers face wait for patient level data from Pfizer and Moderna vaccine trials. 2022; 378:o1731. doi: https://doi.org/10.1136/bmj.o1731

Boschetti, B., & POLI, M. D. (2021). A comparative study on Soft Law: Lessons from the COVID-19 Pandemic. *Cambridge Yearbook of European Legal Studies*, 23, 20 – 53.

Brady, H. E. (2000). Contributions of survey research to political science. *PS: Political Science & Politics*, 33(1), 47 – 58.

Buchanan, L., Bui, Q., & Patel, J. K. (2020). Black Lives Matter May Be the Largest Movement in U.S. History. *The New York Times*. July 3, 2020. Retrieved from: https://www.nytimes.com/interactive/2020/07/03/us/george-floyd-protests-crowd-size.html

Burke, G., Federman, J., Wu, H., Pathi, K., & McGuirk, R. (2022). Police Seize on COVID-19 Tech to Expand Global Surveillance. *AP News*. December 21, 2022. Retrieved from: https://apnews.com/article/technology-police-government-surveillance-covid-19-3f3f348d176bc7152a8cb2dbab2e4cc4

Burni, A., & Tamaki, E. (2021). Populist communication during the Covid-19 pandemic: the case of Brazi's President Bolsonaro. *Partecipazione e Conflitto*, 14(1), 113 – 131.

Bustikova, L., & Babos, P. (2020). Best in Covid: Populists in the time of pandemic. *Politics and Governance*, 8(4), 496 – 508.

CDC. (2021a). COVID-19 hospitalization and death by age. Retrieved from: https://covid.cdc.gov/covid-data-tracker/#hospitalizations_allages

CDC. (2021b). COVID-19 Vaccinations in the United States. Retrieved from: https://covid.cdc.gov/covid-data-tracker/#vaccinations

CDC. (2021c). Science Brief: Obesity, Race/Ethnicity, and COVID-19. Retrieved from: https://www.cdc.gov/coronavirus/2019-ncov/science/science-briefs/obesity-race-ethnicity.html

CDC. (2013). Travelers' Health Most Frequently Asked Questions. Centers for Disease Control and Prevention. May 12, 2013. Retrieved from: https://wwwnc.cdc.gov/travel/page/faq

Center for Systems Science and Engineering. (2023). COVID-19 Dashboard. *John Hopkins University*. March 31, 2023. Retrieved from: https://gisanddata.maps.arcgis.com/apps/dashboards/bda7594740fd40299423467b48e9ecf6

Chee, F. Y. (2020, March 25). Vodafone, Deutsche Telekom, 6 other telcos to help EU track virus. *Reuters.* https://www. reuters.com/article/us-health-coronavirus-telecoms-euidUSKBN21C36G.

Cheng, X. (2021). Soft Law in the prevention and control of the COVID-19 pandemic in China: Between Legality Concerns and Limited Participatory Possibilities. *European Journal of Risk Regulation*, 12(1), 7–25.

Childrens Health Defense Fund. (2022). The COVID Vaccine Mandate for Military Members Might Be the Next One to Fall + More. December 12, 2022. Retrieved from: https://child renshealthdefense.org/defender/bb-covid-vaccine-mandate-military-next-to-fall/

Choi, J. (2021). Fauci: Vaccinated people become 'dead ends' for the coronavirus. *The Hill.* May 16, 2021. Retrieved from: https://thehill.com/homenews/sunday-talk-shows/553773-fauci-vaccinated-people-become-dead-ends-for-the-coronavirus/

Chow, D., & Saliba, E. (2020). Italy has a world-class health system. The coronavirus has pushed it to the breaking point. *NBC News.* March 19, 2020. Retrieved from: https://www.nbcnews.com/ health/health-news/italy-has-world-class-health-system-coronavirus-has-pushed-it-n1162786

Cooper, D., Hickey., S. M., & Zipperer, B. (2022). The value of the federal minimum wage is at its lowest point in 66 years. *Economic Policy Institute.* July 14, 2022. Retrieved from: https://www. epi.org/blog/the-value-of-the-federal-minimum-wage-is-at-its-lowest-point-in-66-years/

Corbet, S. (2021). France's virus pass now required in restaurants, trains. *AP News.* August 9, 2021. Retrieved from: https://apnews.com/article/europe-business-health-france-coronavirus-pandemic-655d8451d7494f8663ce2072e64cf7a6

COVID-19 Global Gender Response Tracker. (2023). *Data Features: Platform.* Retrieved from: https:// data.undp.org/gendertracker/

Crawley, J. (2008). Bailout, plug-in credit a boost for automakers. *Reuters.* October 3, 2008. Retrieved from: https://www.reuters.com/article/retire-us-financial-bailout-autos-idUSTRE4928UE20081003

Csernatoni, R. (2020). New states of emergency: normalizing techno-surveillance in the time of COVID-19. *Global Affairs*, 6(3), 301–310.

Cunha, M. P. E., Berti, M., & Clegg, S. (2021). European social theory reflecting on a time of contagion: a book review essay. *Journal of Political Power*, 14(2), 372–382.

Dados, N., & Connell, R. (2012). The global south. *Contexts*, 11(1), 12–13.

Davidson, H. (2020). Hong Kong using Covid-19 crisis as 'golden opportunity' for crackdown, says arrested leader. *The Guardian.* April 20, 2020. Retrieved from: https://www.theguardian.com/ world/2020/apr/20/hong-kong-using-covid-19-crisis-as-golden-opportunity-for-crackdown-says-ar rested-leader

Davies, H., Hjorth, L., Andrejevic, M., Richardson, I., & DeSouza, R. (2023). QR codes during the pandemic: Seamful quotidian placemaking. *Convergence*, 13548565231160623.

Dincer, D., & Gocer, O. (2021). Quarantine hotels: The adaptation of hotels for quarantine use in Australia. *Buildings*, 11(12), 617.

Doffman, Z. (2020). Coronavirus Spy Drones Hit Europe: This is How They're Now Used. *Forbes.* March 16, 2020. Retrieved from: https://www.forbes.com/sites/zakdoffman/2020/03/16/coronavi rus-spy-drones-hit-europe-police-surveillance-enforces-new-covid-19-lockdowns/?sh= 2c4639287471

DW News. (2020a). Germany to pump in €3 billion in ailing car industry. *DW News.* November 18, 2020. Retrieved from: https://www.dw.com/en/germany-to-pump-additional-3billion-in-ailing-au tomotive-industry/a-55641102

DW News. (2020b). France to pump €8 billion into car industry. *DW News.* May 27, 2020. Retrieved from: https://www.dw.com/en/france-unveils-stimulus-plan-worth-8-billion-for-car-industry/a-53578294

Eberl, J. M., Huber, R. A., & Greussing, E. (2021). From populism to the "plandemic": Why populists believe in COVID-19 conspiracies. *Journal of Elections, Public Opinion and Parties*, 31(sup1), 272–284.

Edgell, A. B., Lachapelle, J., Lührmann, A., & Maerz, S. F. (2021). Pandemic backsliding: Violations of democratic standards during Covid-19. *Social Science & Medicine*, 285, 114244.

Eichler, J., & Sonkar, S. (2021). Challenging Absolute Executive Powers in Times of Corona: Re-Examining Constitutional Courts and the Collective Right to Public Contestation as Instruments of Institutional Control. *Review of Economics and Political Science*, 6(1), 3–23.

Eliantonio, M., Korkea-Aho, E., & Vaughan, S. (2021). EJRR Special Issue Editorial: COVID-19 and soft law: is soft law pandemic-proof? *European Journal of Risk Regulation*, 12(1), 1–6.

European Center for Not-for-Profit Law. (2023). COVID-19 Civic Freedom Tracker. Retrieved from: https://www.icnl.org/covid19tracker/?location=&issue=10&date=&type=

European Commission. (2020, November 11). Regulation of the European parliament and of the council on serious cross-border threats to health and repealing Decision No 1082/2013/ EU. EUR-Lex – 52020PC0727 – EN – EUR-Lex (europa.eu)

Ferretti, L., Wymant, C., Kendall, M., Zhao, L., Nurtay, A., Abeler-Dörner, L., & Hinch, R. (2020). Quantifying SARS-CoV-2 transmission suggests epidemic control with digital contact tracing. *Science*, 368(6491), eabb6936.

Figus, A., & de Serio, L. (2020). Covid 19 between globalisation, mobility and complexity. *Geopolitical, Social Security and Freedom Journal*, 3(2), 2–13.

Foa, R. S., & Mounk, Y. (2016). The danger of deconsolidation: The democratic disconnect. *Journal of democracy*, 27(3), 5–17.

Foodandwaterwatch. (2021). The Economic Cost of Food Monopolies: The Grocery Cartels. Issue Brief. November 2021. Retrieved from: https://www.foodandwaterwatch.org/wp-content/uploads/2021/11/IB_2111_FoodMonoSeries1-SUPERMARKETS-V2FINAL.pdf

Foucault, M. (2019). The History of Sexuality. London: Penguin.

Fourcade, M., & Healy, K. (2017). Seeing like a market. *Socio-Economic Review* 15(1),9–29.

Fraiman, J., Erviti, J., Jones, M., Greenland, S., Whelan, P., Kaplan, R. M., & Doshi, P. (2022). Serious adverse events of special interest following mRNA COVID-19 vaccination in randomized trials in adults. *Vaccine*, 40(40), 5798–5805.

Garrett, P. M. (2022). 'Surveillance Capitalism, COVID-19 and social work': A note on uncertain future(s). *The British Journal of Social Work*, 52(3), 1747–1764.

Gautret, P., Botelho-Nevers, E., Brouqui, P., & Parola, P. (2012). The spread of vaccine-preventable diseases by international travellers: a public-health concern. *Clinical microbiology and infection*, 18, 77–84.

Gitlin, J. M. (2021). Traffic congestion dropped by 73 percent in 2020 due to the pandemic. *ArsTechnica.* March 9, 2021. Retrieved from: https://arstechnica.com/cars/2021/03/covid-19-caused-big-drops-in-city-congestion-in-2020-study-finds/

Glasius, M. (2018). What authoritarianism is... and is not: a practice perspective. *International Affairs*, 94(3), 515–533.

Glasius, M., & Michaelsen, M. (2018). Authoritarian practices in the digital age. Illiberal and authoritarian practices in the digital sphere—prologue. *International Journal of Communication*, 12, 19.

Google. (2020). Exposure Notification: Bluetooth Specification. April 2020, v1.2. Retrieved from: https://covid19-static.cdn-apple.com/applications/covid19/current/static/contact-tracing/pdf/Ex posureNotification-BluetoothSpecificationv1.2.pdf?1

Government of the Czech Republic. (2020a). The government has decided to extend restrictions on public movement until 1 April, and has also approved further steps to support employers. Press Advisory. March 24, 2020. Retrieved from: https://www.vlada.cz/en/media-centrum/aktualne/the-government-has-decided-to-extend-restrictions-on-public-movement-until-1-april-and-has-also-ap proved-further-steps-to-support-employers-180587/

Government of the Czech Republic. (2020b). Restriction of free movement, retail sale and services extended to 11 April; smart-quarantine project launched. Press Advisory. March 30, 2020. Retrieved from: https://www.vlada.cz/en/media-centrum/aktualne/restriction-of-free-movement-retail-sale-and-services-extended-to-11-april-smart-quarantine-project-launched-180852/

Government of the Czech Republic. (2020c). Exercising alone to be allowed without face masks. Government to allow some shops to re-open from Thursday. Press Advisory. April 6, 2020. Retrieved from: https://www.vlada.cz/en/media-centrum/aktualne/exercising-alone-to-be-al lowed-without-face-masks-government-to-allow-some-shops-to-re-open-from-thursday-180926/

Government of the Czech Republic. (2020d). Resolution No. 1113. October 30, 2020. Retrieved from: https://www.vlada.cz/assets/media-centrum/aktualne/19_R_free-movement_1113_30102020.pdf

Government of the Netherlands. (2017). Vaccinations. Netherlands Worldwide. Retrieved from: https://www.netherlandsworldwide.nl/travel-abroad/vaccinations

Gray, T. (2021). Voice: You won't get the vaccine? How do you live with knowing you're harming others? *The Desert Sun.* February 10, 2021. Retrieved from: https://eu.desertsun.com/story/opin ion/contributors/valley-voice/2021/03/06/voice-criminally-charge-covid-19-vaccine-refuseniks-anti-vaxxers/4570849001/

Grogan, J. (2022). Impact of COVID-19 measures on fundamental rights and democracy. European Parliament's special committee on the COVID-19 pandemic: lessons learned and recommendations for the future (COVI). November 2022. Retrieved from: https://www.europarl.europa.eu/RegData/etudes/STUD/2022/734010/IPOL_STU(2022)734010_EN.pdf

Gupta, D. (2022). COVID-19 Effects on Grocery Business: How to Survive the Phase? August, 8, 2022. Retrieved from: https://appinventiv.com/blog/coronavirus-effects-on-grocery-business/

Hale, T., Angrist, N., Goldszmidt, R., Kira, B., Petherick, A., Phillips, T., & Tatlow, H. (2021). A global panel database of pandemic policies (Oxford COVID-19 Government Response Tracker). *Nature Human Behaviour*, 5(4), 529-538.

Han, S. M., & Han, K. (2023). Authoritarian leaders, economic hardship, and inequality. *Democratization*, 1–21. DOI: 10.1080/13510347.2023.2209022

Hays, J. N. (2009). *The Burdens of Disease.* Rutgers University Press.

Heller, H. (2015). Authoritarian liberalism. *European Law Journal*, 21 (3), 295.

Helmore, E. (2023). US guarantees all deposits after Silicon Valley Bank collapse, as Biden promises action. *The Guardian.* March 12, 2023. Retrieved from: https://www.theguardian.com/business/2023/mar/12/silicon-valley-bank-collapse-no-bailout-janet-yellen

Hoepman, J. H. (2020). Stop the Apple and Google contact tracing platform (or be ready to ditch your smartphone). https://blog.xot.nl/2020/04/11/stop-the-apple-and-google-contact-tracing-platf orm-or-be-ready-to-ditch-your-smartphone/.

Holder, J. (2023). Tracking Coronavirus Vaccinations Around the World. *The New York Times.* March 13, 2023. Retrieved from: https://www.nytimes.com/interactive/2021/world/covid-vaccinations-tracker.html

Holmes, O. (2020). Israeli spies source up to 100,000 coronavirus tests in covert mission. *The Guardian.* March 19, 2020. Retrieved from: https://www.theguardian.com/world/2020/mar/19/israeli-spies-source-100000-coronavirus-tests-covert-foreign-mission

Horsley, S. (2020). 3 Months Of Hell: U.S. Economy Drops 32.9% In Worst GDP Report Ever. *NPR News.* July 30, 2020. Retrieved from: https://www.npr.org/sections/coronavirus-live-updates/2020/07/30/896714437/3-months-of-hell-u-s-economys-worst-quarter-ever

Hrushka, A. (2023). Silicon Valley Bank investors sue collapsed firm's CEO, CFO. *BankingDive.* March 14, 2023. Retrieved from: https://www.bankingdive.com/news/silicon-valley-bank-investors-sue-collapse-ceo-cfo-greg-becker-daniel-beck/644951/

Human Mortality Database. (2023). Downloading the HMD in zipped data files. Retrieved from: https://www.mortality.org/Data/ZippedDataFiles

Hunte, S. A., Pierre, K., Rose, R. S., & Simeon, D. T. (2020). Health systems' resilience: COVID-19 response in Trinidad and Tobago. *The American journal of tropical medicine and hygiene*, 103(2), 590.

Inman, P. (2020). The huge coronavirus bailouts will need to be paid back. Or will they? *The Guardian.* March 28, 2020. Retrieved from: https://www.theguardian.com/business/2020/mar/28/coronavirus-bailouts-need-to-be-paid-back-or-do-they

Jefferson, T., Dooley, L., Ferroni, E., Al-Ansary, L. A., van Driel, M. L., Bawazeer, G. A., Jones, M. A., Hoffmann, T. C., Clark, J., Beller, E. M., Glasziou, P. P., & Conly, J. M. (2023). Physical interventions to interrupt or reduce the spread of respiratory viruses. *Cochrane database of systematic reviews.* Onlinefirst. https://doi.org/10.1002/14651858.CD006207.pub6

Johnson, K. (2020). Apple and Google partner on Bluetooth interoperability for COVID-19 tracing apps. VentureBeat. April 10, 2020. Retrieved from: https://venturebeat.com/mobile/apple-and-google-partner-on-bluetooth-interoperability-for-covid-19-tracing-apps/

Johnson, M., & Ghiglione, D. (2020). Coronavirus 'tsunami' pushes Italy's hospitals to breaking point. *Financial Times.* March 11, 2020. Retrieved from: https://www.ft.com/content/34f25036-62f4-11ea-a6cd-df28cc3c6a68

Katawazi, M. (2021). Ontario reveals vaccine passport system for restaurants, gyms and theatres. Here's what you need to know. *Toronto CTVNews.* September 1, 2021. Retrieved from: https://toronto.ctvnews.ca/ontario-reveals-vaccine-passport-system-for-restaurants-gyms-and-theatres-here-s-what-you-need-to-know-1.5569198

Kelloway, C. (2022). U.S. Food Prices Are Up. Are the Food Corporations to Blame for Taking Advantage? *Time.* January 14, 2022. Retrieved from: https://time.com/6139127/u-s-food-prices-monopoly/

Kimball, S. (2023). The Covid pandemic drives Pfizer's 2022 revenue to a record $100 billion. *CNBC.* January 31, 2023. Retrieved from: https://www.cnbc.com/2023/01/31/the-covid-pandemic-drives-pfizers-2022-revenue-to-a-record-100-billion.html

Kisielinski, K., Hirsch, O., Wagner, S., Wojtasik, B., Funken, S., Klosterhalfen, B., Manna, S. K., Prescher, A., Sukul, P., & Sönnichsen, A. (2023). Physio-metabolic and clinical consequences of wearing face masks-Systematic review with meta-analysis and comprehensive evaluation. *Frontiers in Public Health.* 11. https://doi.org/10.3389/fpubh.2023.1125150

Kivotidis, D. (2021). *Dictatorship: New Trajectories in Law.* London: Routledge.

Krishnarajan, S. (2022). Rationalizing democracy: The perceptual bias and (Un) democratic behavior. *American Political Science Review*, 1–23. doi:10.1017/S0003055422000806

Kropotkin, P. (2015). The Conquest of Bread. London: Penguin.

Kumar, A. (2023). Twitter Files 17: A chilling cocktail of censorship and Hinduphobia. *The Sunday Guardian.* March 11, 2023. Retrieved from: https://sundayguardianlive.com/opinion/twitter-files-17-a-chilling-cocktail-of-censorship-and-hinduphobia

Laclau, E. (1990). *New Reflections on the Revolution of Our Time.* London: Verso.

Laris, M., & Aratani, L. (2021). Taxpayers spent billions bailing out airlines. Did the industry hold up its end of the deal? *The Washington Post.* December 14, 2021. Retrieved from: https://www.washingtonpost.com/transportation/2021/12/14/airline-bailout-covid-flights/

Lazzarato, M. (2002). From biopower to biopolitics. *Pli: The Warwick Journal of Philosophy*, 13(8), 1–6.

Lee, J. W. (2021). Government bailouts of airlines in the COVID-19 crisis: Improving transparency in international air transport. *Journal of International Economic Law*, 24(4), 703–723.

Lewkowicz, J., Woźniak, M., & Wrzesiński, M. (2022). COVID-19 and erosion of democracy. *Economic Modelling*, 106, 105682.

Little, A., & Meng, A. (2023). Subjective and Objective Measurement of Democratic Backsliding. January 17, 2023. Available at *SSRN:* https://ssrn.com/abstract=4327307 or http://dx.doi.org/10.2139/ssrn.4327307

Linthicum, K. (2020). The whole world is spending to fight coronavirus. In Mexico, the leftist president is making cuts. *The Los Angeles Times.* May 13, 2020. Retrieved from: https://www.latimes.com/world-nation/story/2020-05-13/mexico-poised-to-plunge-into-its-worse-recession-in-recent-memory-moves-to-reopen-parts-of-its-economy

Liu, J., Wei, H., & He, D. (2023). Differences in case-fatality-rate of emerging SARS-CoV-2 variants. *Public Health in Practice*, 5, 100350.

Llanos, M., & Weber, C. T. Court–Executive Relations during the COVID-19 Pandemic: Business as Usual or Democratic Backsliding? In Llanos, M., & Marsteintredet, L. (eds.). *Latin America in Times of Turbulence.* Routledge. pp. 128–147.

Lovelace Jr. B. (2021). Pfizer CEO says people who spread misinformation on Covid vaccines are 'criminals'. *CNBC.* November 9, 2021. Retrieved from: https://www.cnbc.com/2021/11/09/covid-vaccines-pfizer-ceo-says-people-who-spread-misinformation-on-shots-are-criminals.html

MacAskill, E., Borger, J., Hopkins, N., Davies, N., & Ball, J. (2013). GCHQ taps fibre-optic cables for secret access to world's communications. *The Guardian.* June 21, 2013. Retrieved from: https://www.theguardian.com/uk/2013/jun/21/gchq-cables-secret-world-communications-nsa

Marquardt, K. (2023). V-Dem Methodology. Retrieved from: https://www.v-dem.net/about/v-dem-project/methodology/

Mason, L., Wronski, J., & Kane, J. V. (2021). Activating animus: The uniquely social roots of Trump support. *American Political Science Review*, 115(4), 1508–1516.

McKinsey & Company (2022). The next horizon for grocery e-commerce: Beyond the pandemic bump. April 29, 2022. Retrieved from: https://www.mckinsey.com/industries/retail/our-insights/the-next-horizon-for-grocery-ecommerce-beyond-the-pandemic-bump

Miani, A., Burgio, E., Piscitelli, P., Lauro, R., & Colao, A. (2020). The Italian war-like measures to fight coronavirus spreading: Re-open closed hospitals now. *EClinicalMedicine*, 21. doi: https://doi.org/10.1016/j.eclinm.2020.100320

Moultan, D. (2023). How Leftists Became Big Pharma's Shock Troops. *CompactMag.* May 10, 2023. Retrieved from: https://compactmag.com/article/how-leftists-became-big-pharma-s-shock-troops

Mudde, C. (2004). The Populist Zeitgeist. *Government and Opposition*, 39(4), 541–563.

Mulligan, C. B., & Arnott, R. D. (2022). Non-COVID excess deaths, 2020–21: collateral damage of policy choices? (No. w30104). *National Bureau of economic research.* Working Paper 30104. Doi: 10.3386/w30104

Mutikani, L. (2021). U.S. economy contracted 19.2% during COVID-19 pandemic recession. *Reuters.* July 29, 2021. Retrieved from: https://www.reuters.com/business/us-economy-contracted-192-during-covid-19-pandemic-recession-2021-07-29/

The New York Times. (2019). Total Surveillance Is Not What America Signed Up For. The Editorial Board. *The New York Times.* December 21, 2019. Retrieved from: https://www.nytimes.com/interactive/2019/12/21/opinion/location-data-privacy-rights.html

Norris, P. (2011). *Democratic deficit: Critical citizens revisited.* Cambridge: Cambridge University Press.

Norwegian Institute of Public Health. (2011). Africa – travel vaccination advice. Retrieved from: https://www.fhi.no/en/id/vaccines/vaccines-overview/world/africa-travel-vaccination-advice/

Oxfam International. (2022). Ten richest men double their fortunes in pandemic while incomes of 99 percent of humanity fall. Press Release. January 17, 2022. Retrieved from: https://www.oxfam.org/en/press-releases/ten-richest-men-double-their-fortunes-pandemic-while-incomes-99-percent-humanity

Oxfam International (2021). Not in this Together: How Supermarkets Became Pandemic Winners While Women Workers are Losing Out. June 2021. Retrieved from: https://oxfamilibrary.openrepository.com/bitstream/handle/10546/621194/bp-not-in-this-together-220621-en.pdf?sequence=22

Perello, L., & Navia, P. (2023). Conditional Cash Transfers and Voting for Incumbents under Democratic Backsliding: The Case of Honduras's Bono 10,000. *Bulletin of Latin American Research.* Online first. https://doi.org/10.1111/blar.13463

Pervou, I. (2022). COVID-19: Introducing a sliding scale between legality and scientific knowledge. *Global Constitutionalism,* 1–12. doi:10.1017/S2045381722000260

Pezzullo, A. M., Axfors, C., Contopoulos-Ioannidis, D. G., Apostolatos, A., & Ioannidis, J. P. (2023). Age-stratified infection fatality rate of COVID-19 in the non-elderly population. *Environmental Research,* 216, 114655.

Phartiyal, S. (2020). India makes government tracing app mandatory for all workers. *Reuters.* May 2, 2020. Retrieved from: https://www.reuters.com/article/health-coronavirus-india-app-idUSL1N2CK01S

Phillips, M. (2020). How the Government Pulls Coronavirus Relief Money Out of Thin Air. *The New York Times.* April 15, 2020. Retrieved from: https://www.nytimes.com/2020/04/15/business/coronavirus-stimulus-money.html

Pilz, S., Theiler-Schwetz, V., Trummer, C., Krause, R., & Ioannidis, J. P. (2022). SARS-CoV-2 reinfections: Overview of efficacy and duration of natural and hybrid immunity. *Environmental Research,* 209, 112911.

Raker, C. (2022). QR codes to enter stores? Dutch retail willing to implement this and more. *DutchReview.* January 5, 2022. Retrieved from: https://dutchreview.com/news/qr-codes-to-enter-stores-dutch-retail-willing-to-implement-this/

Rasmussen Reports. (2023). COVID-19: Democratic Voters Support Harsh Measures Against Unvaccinated. January 13, 2022. Retrieved from: https://www.rasmussenreports.com/public_content/politics/partner_surveys/jan_2022/covid_19_democratic_voters_support_harsh_measures_against_unvaccinated

Recine, C. (2020). Black dye and drones – English police bemuse public with coronavirus response. *Reuters.* March 28, 2020. Retrieved from: https://www.reuters.com/article/uk-health-coronavirus-britain-police-idUKKBN21F0LA

Reuters. (2021). Bulgaria makes COVID 'health pass' obligatory for leisure activities. *Reuters.* October 19, 2021. Retrieved from: https://www.reuters.com/world/europe/bulgaria-makes-covid-health-pass-obligatory-leisure-activities-2021-10-19/

Reuters. (2020). German carmakers, government to look at boosting suppliers' equity capital. September 8, 2020. *Reuters.* Retrieved from: https://www.reuters.com/article/uk-germany-autos-idUKKBN25Z364

Ringe, N., & Renno, L. (2023). *Populists and the Pandemic How Populists Around the World Responded to COVID-19.* London: Routledge.

Romano, V., Ancillotti, M., Mascalzoni, D., & Biasiotto, R. (2022). Italians locked down: people's responses to early COVID-19 pandemic public health measures. *Humanities and Social Sciences Communications*, 9(1), 1–9.

Romm, T., Dwoskin, E., & Timberg, C. (2020). U.S. government, tech industry discussing ways to use smartphone location data to combat coronavirus. *The Washington Post.* March 17, 2020. Retrieved from: https://www.washingtonpost.com/technology/2020/03/17/white-house-location-data-coronavirus/

Samuels, D. J. (2023). The International Context of Democratic Backsliding: Rethinking the Role of Third Wave "Prodemocracy" Global Actors. *Perspectives on Politics*, 1–12. https://doi.org/10.1017/S1537592722003334

Satter, R. (2020). To keep COVID-19 patients home, some U.S. states weigh house arrest tech. *Reuters.* May 7, 2020. Retrieved from: https://www.reuters.com/article/us-health-coronavirus-quarantine-tech-idUKKBN22J1U8

Schemmel, A. (2023). Switzerland not recommending COVID vaccines, even for high risk individuals, during spring and summer. *ABC 13 News.* April 10, 2023. Retrieved from: https://wlos.com/news/nation-world/switzerland-not-recommending-covid-vaccines-even-for-high-risk-individuals-during-spring-and-summer

Schengen Visa Info. (2021). Travellers Vaccinated With Russian, Chinese & Indian Vaccines May Be Unable to Enter Majority of EU Countries. June 15, 2021. Retrieved from: https://www.schengenvisainfo.com/news/travellers-vaccinated-with-russian-chinese-indian-vaccines-may-be-unable-to-enter-majority-of-eu-countries/#google_vignette

Scherer, S., & Gordon, J. (2021). Canada imposes COVID-19 vaccine mandate on federal workers, transportation. *Reuters.* October 6, 2021. Retrieved from: https://www.reuters.com/world/americas/unvaccinated-federal-workers-canada-will-be-put-unpaid-leave-globe-mail-2021-10-06/

Schubert, L., Dye, T. R., & Zeigler, H. (2015). The Irony of Democracy: An Uncommon Introduction to American Politics. Boston: Cengage Learning.

Sharon, T. (2021). Blind-sided by privacy? Digital contact tracing, the Apple/Google API and big tech's newfound role as global health policy makers. *Ethics and Information Technology*, 23(Suppl 1), 45–57.

Shellenberger, M. (2023). 'Censorship-industrial complex' uses gov't power to threaten democracy. *The New York Post.* March 13, 2023. Retrieved from: https://nypost.com/2023/03/10/censorship-industrial-complex-uses-power-to-threaten-democracy/

Shepardson, D., & Rucinski, T. (2020). U.S. Senate approves big rescue for struggling aviation sector. *Reuters.* March 25, 2020. Retrieved from: https://www.reuters.com/article/us-health-coronavirus-usa-bill-idUSKBN21C24T

Shrestha, N. K., Burke, P. C., Nowacki, A. S., Terpeluk, P., & Gordon, S. M. (2021). Necessity of COVID-19 vaccination in previously infected individuals. *MedRxiv*, 2021–06.

Singh, A., & Tembo, S. (2022). Constitutionalism and public health emergencies: covid-19 regulations in south africa and the constitutional and human rights slippery slope. *Obiter*, 43(1), 152–166.

Stephens, P. (2022). Food giants reap enormous profits during times of crisis. *PhysOrg*. June 14, 2022. Retrieved from: https://phys.org/news/2022-06-food-giants-reap-enormous-profits.html

Stewart, E. (2023). Is this a bailout? *Vox*. March 13, 2023. Retrieved from: https://www.vox.com/money/2023/3/13/23638417/svb-bank-bailout-signature-fed-fdic-treasury-janet-yellen

Svolik, M. W. 2019. Polarization versus democracy. *Journal of Democracy*, 30(3), 20–32.

Sweeney, Y. (2020). Tracking the debate on COVID-19 surveillance tools. *Nature Machine Intelligence*, 2(6), 301–304.

Taddonio, P. (2020). 18 Years Old and on a Ventilator With COVID-19. *PBS Frontline*. May 19, 2020. Retrieved from: https://www.pbs.org/wgbh/frontline/article/teenager-on-a-ventilator-with-coronavirus/

Treguer, F. (2020). The State and Digital Surveillance in Times of the Covid-19 Pandemic, CERI's Series on the COVID-19 Pandemic. SciencesPo – Center for International Studies, June 1. Accessed on 16.06.2022, at: https://www.sciencespo.fr/ceri/en/content/state-and-digital-surveillance-times-covid-19-pandemic.

Treguer, F. (2021). The Virus of Surveillance: How the COVID-19 pandemic is fuelling technologies of control. *Political Anthropological Research on International Social Sciences (PARISS)*, 2(1), 16–46.

U.S. State Department. (2021). Chile 2021 Human Rights Report. Executive Summary. Retrieved from: https://www.state.gov/wp-content/uploads/2022/03/313615_CHILE-2021-HUMAN-RIGHTS-REPORT.pdf

van der Zwet, K., Barros, A. I., van Engers, T. M., & Sloot, P. M. (2022). Emergence of protests during the COVID-19 pandemic: quantitative models to explore the contributions of societal conditions. *Humanities and Social Sciences Communications*, 9(1).

Venkatesh, N. (2021). Surveillance Capitalism: a Marx-inspired account. *Philosophy*, 96(3), 359–385.

Viga Gaier, R. & Rochabrun, M. (2020). Brazil says airline bailout settled, but carriers say talks ongoing. *NASDAQ*. May 15, 2020. Retrieved from: https://www.nasdaq.com/articles/brazil-says-airline-bailout-settled-but-carriers-say-talks-ongoing-2020-05-15

Walder, D., & Lust, E. (2018). Unwelcome Change: Coming to Terms with Democratic Backsliding. *Annual Review of Political Science*, 21(1), 93–113.

Wilkinson, M. A. (2022). Authoritarian liberalism and the transformation of modern Europe: Rejoinder. *European Law Open*, 1(1), 191–208.

Wilkinson, M. A. (2021). Authoritarian Liberalism and the Transformation of Modern Europe. Oxford: Oxford University Press.

Winblad, U., Swenning, A. K., & Spangler, D. (2022). Soft law and individual responsibility: a review of the Swedish policy response to COVID-19. *Health Economics, Policy and Law*, 17(1), 48–61.

Wishnick, E. (2021). China and Russia: Vaccine Competitors or Partners? February 23, 2021. Retrieved from: https://thediplomat.com/2021/02/china-and-russia-vaccine-competitors-or-partners/

Wolkenstein, F. (2022). What is democratic backsliding. *Consetellations*. Onlinefirst. https://doi.org/10.1111/1467-8675.12627

Woodward, C., & Yen, H. (2021). AP FACT CHECK: Biden goes too far in assurances on vaccines. *AP News*. July 22, 2021. Retrieved from: https://apnews.com/article/joe-biden-business-health-government-and-politics-coronavirus-pandemic-46a270ce0f681caa7e4143e2ae9a0211

World Health Organization. (2023a). Measles, Key Facts. March 20, 2023. Retrieved from: https://www.who.int/news-room/fact-sheets/detail/measles

World Health Organization. (2023b). WHO Coronavirus (COVID-19) Dashboard. Retrieved from: https://covid19.who.int/

World Health Organization. (2022a). Global expenditure on health: Rising to the pandemic's challenges. Retrieved from: https://www.who.int/publications/i/item/9789240064911

World Health Organization. (2022b). COVID-19 pandemic triggers 25 % increase in prevalence of anxiety and depression worldwide. March 2, 2022. Retrieved from: https://www.who.int/news/item/02-03-2022-covid-19-pandemic-triggers-25-increase-in-prevalence-of-anxiety-and-depression-worldwide

World Health Organization. (2021a). WHO-convened global study of origins of SARS-CoV-2: China Part. February 10, 2021. Retrieved from: https://www.who.int/publications/i/item/who-convened-global-study-of-origins-of-sars-cov-2-china-part

World Health Organization (2021b). Weekly epidemiological update on COVID-19 – 30 March 2021. Retrieved from: https://www.who.int/publications/m/item/weekly-epidemiological-update-on-covid-19--31-march-2021

World Health Organization. (2021c). Global expenditure on health: Public spending on the rise? Retrieved from: https://files.aho.afro.who.int/afahobckpcontainer/production/files/2_Global_expenditure_on_health_Public_spending_on_the_rise.pdf

World Health Organization (2020a). WHO Director-General's opening remarks at the media briefing on COVID-19 – 11 March 2020. March 11, 2020. Retrieved from: https://www.who.int/director-general/speeches/detail/who-director-general-s-opening-remarks-at-the-media-briefing-on-covid-19--11-march-2020

World Health Organization (2020b). Coronavirus disease 2019 (COVID-19), Situation Report – 40. February 29, 2020. Retrieved from: https://www.who.int/docs/default-source/coronaviruse/situation-reports/20200229-sitrep-40-covid-19.pdf?sfvrsn=7203e653_2

World Health Organization (2020c). Rational use of personal protective equipment for coronavirus disease 2019 (COVID-19). February 27, 2020. Retrieved from: https://apps.who.int/iris/bitstream/handle/10665/331215/WHO-2019-nCov-IPCPPE_use-2020.1-eng.pdf

World Health Organization (2020d). Coronavirus disease 2019 (COVID-19), Situation Report – 101. April 30, 2020. Retrieved from: https://www.who.int/docs/default-source/coronaviruse/situation-reports/20200430-sitrep-101-covid-19.pdf?sfvrsn=2ba4e093_2

World Health Organization. (2020e). At least 80 million children under one at risk of diseases such as diphtheria, measles and polio as COVID-19 disrupts routine vaccination efforts, warn Gavi, WHO and UNICEF. May 22, 2020. Retrieved from: https://www.who.int/news/item/22-05-2020-at-least-80-million-children-under-one-at-risk-of-diseases-such-as-diphtheria-measles-and-polio-as-covid-19-disrupts-routine-vaccination-efforts-warn-gavi-who-and-unicef

Wuttke, A., Gavras, K., & Schoen, H. (2022). Have Europeans grown tired of democracy? New evidence from eighteen consolidated democracies, 1981 – 2018. *British Journal of Political Science*, 52(1), 416 – 428.

Zorina, A., Bélanger, F., Kumar, N., & Clegg, S. (2021). Watchers, watched, and watching in the digital age: reconceptualization of information technology monitoring as complex action nets. *Organization Science*, 32(6), 1571 – 1596.

Zuboff, S. (2019). *The Age of Surveillance Capitalism: The Fight for a Human Future at the New Frontier of Power.* New York City: Hachette.

Index

https://doi.org/10.1515/9783111345703-009